Norma Jean's Sun

Kris Courtney

Edited by Heidi Connolly, Harvard Girl Word Services, *www.harvardgirledits.com*

All artwork, Cover design and content created by Kris Courtney.

ISBN-10: 0578020599

ISBN-13: 978-0578020594

This novel is dedicated to the memory of my mother and grandmother.

They were incredible women.

The characters in this book are based on my recollections and in no way represent objective truth. Therefore, any resemblance to persons living or dead, with the exception of historical figures, places, and events is purely coincidental. Any similarities of locations, and/or institutions in this book to actual places or organizations are purely accidental. Some of the events depicted in this story are true; however, the story itself is fictional. This book is intended as a fictionalized account of my own life experiences and should not be considered an account of fact or for any other reason than entertainment.

AUTHOR'S NOTE

I give thanks for the wealth of experience life has offered me and for the awareness, understanding, and patience it has brought with it. Even though the pages that follow will tell a story of a life of trial and pain, the resultant insight and knowledge has brought greater understanding and peace as well. I can now say with complete assurance that my deeds are done, my heart is safe, and my soul is clean. Through all the resentments and challenges, there always ran an undercurrent of hope that change was possible; this hope kept me connected to a life that has been wealthy and wise even in times of poverty and despair.

Chapter 1

SETTING SIDE OF THE TRACKS

The morning opens and a mist of innocence appears across the countryside, telling us the day is new. The feeling of hope and love and the humble awareness of duty is clear, if only for a moment. It is that inspiration that follows us into a small town, where we are awakened by a cool frost to the laughter of children playing on this Sunday morning.

Driving through the fall of 1928, the trees cover the hillside; it is as if a collection of sponges and rags dipped in paint have been thrown against the ground, each one offering an array of amber, gold, ruby, and sienna, like purple diamonds sparkling in the morning sun.

Robert Parker and his faithful wife Mary are on their way to see Mary's sister Gladys and her children to invite them to church. Knowing the invitation will be gracefully declined, their feelings of commitment and loyalty continue to send them on this journey every week.

"Settle down now, children. You need to be on your best behavior when we get there…and Johnny, you will not get those pants dirty today, you hear me?!" Mary says this sternly but lovingly, looking back at her children in the back seat.

"Yes, Mother," Johnny replies, already squirming in his creased trousers.

Each child represents the achievement and a way of life reflected by the times. The depression has not yet come to America, and the belief that hard work brings rewards is still a valid one. In this family we have six children. John, or Johnny, Bill, Tom, Benny, Jack, and Martha. Bill is the oldest and strongest, but each one is just as spirited and fun-loving as the next. Though Martha is the only girl, she can stand toe to toe with the boys just fine. Never is there a question of equality or justice for one at the expense of all. Each knows his and her place, what is acceptable and what is not. That is the way their parents taught them and they do what they are told.

As the car enters the long drive, the grass is noticeably high, the grounds showing signs of neglect. The flowers have softened below their once high, proud stance of beauty. You can see this home had been cared for with love and diligence in the past, that it had stood tall and firm, but was now shadowed with stains. The broken glass that cloaks the upstairs window tells the story of an empty future, or a past that need not be spoken. Though the fence around the side yard still stands strong, it needs a painting, and the swing set is rusted with neglect. It speaks in the wind, claiming its independence and its loneliness.

* * *

As this journey begins, I recount the tale from this same old house resting on the hill. It offers a view of the carnival that comes every year to this small town and sets up just across the tracks. My pallet is dry now; the colors are gone. The rain has washed away most of the signs that once stood for a prosperous home and family. My grave is waiting. The dreams that once filled my head with images of world unity, hope, and companionship are gone. The saga told through my canvas has only drawn darker as the years have passed, bitter days into bitter cold nights. All that comes to me now are glimpses of the faces that have graced my soul.

* * *

"Hello, Mary. Robert, you look so handsome. Come in, come in," Gladys said, greeting her family at the door.

The children follow close behind, eager to get into the house that always has fresh-baked pies or treats. It has been two long years since this a child laughed or gasped in excitement here.

"Gladys, you look lovely this fine morning," Robert said. "I am still not sure why I didn't marry you instead of your Sister." Robert loved to jest.

The women turned and smiled at the joke, chuckling with polite laughter.

"Where is Hildreth?" Johnny asked loudly, to be sure he'd be heard above the adult talk.

"She must be upstairs, honey," said Gladys, "Go up and see if you can find her. Be careful, though—all of you, and stay in the side yard if you go out... I mean it!"

"Yes, Aunt Gladys," the children said in unison, and ran up to find their cousin.

The void they left was instantly filled with concern and a sense of distraction...discomfort. The adults went into the kitchen, each searching for the exact moment to speak, each reaching for a word of comfort that might ease the burden of pain in Gladys' heart. Mary wrapped her arm around Gladys to connect and absorb the impact. "How are you doing, dear? Is it getting any easier? You know we would love to take you with us today. The preacher asks about you all the time and prays for your happiness."

Sorrow and the weight of a ton of granite could be heard in Gladys' reply. "My heart and soul are better, but I'm not ready to go just yet. I look forward to these Sundays with the children. It gives me a direction and fills the empty space left behind, if even for only a day. Your children are mine, too, and I love them all so dearly, Mary, Robert. I just need a little more time."

Knowing the only thing they had to offer was silence and empathy, Robert and Mary hugged Gladys and each other. For a while the only sound was the ticking of the clock on the wall as the adults settled into their memories.

* * *

The trail of heartaches, glory, and achievements that each of our players brings to this tale defines a pattern of character that will last a century. The little house on the hill that oversees a collection of roofs below gives sight every year to a pallet of change, change felt by all who are watching, watching for the good and evil spirits who battle for souls once touched only by divine innocence.

* * *

Two years ago on a humid summer day, Gladys' husband Larry came home for lunch. Larry had a good job working for the local rail yard, a job considered by many as one which would ensure him a lifetime of financial security. However, on this day, lifetime and security would leave his grasp and never return. For this is the day his children of two became one.

Larry came up the road to his house and waved to his friends out the window of his truck. He noticed a man, walking alone. The man had a harsh look about him—unusual, because work was slim for drifters and it was summer. Larry was used to seeing rail-jumpers at the yard, but had never seen this one before. As Larry pulled into the drive, he felt the house's silence and the idea that something was wrong swept through him. The feeling was so strong it forced a gasp from deep in his chest. It was a feeling he had never felt before. He stopped the truck and walked feverishly towards the house, not taking the time to close the car door. He was met on the porch by Gladys, in tears, her eyes swollen and her hands shaking. "He's gone Larry…he took him away and I can't find him." Gladys voice shattered; she was no longer able to speak.

7

"What, woman? What are you saying, Gladys? Where is Doyle? Where is Hildreth… Where are the children, dammit?"

When he got no answer, Larry walked through the house in terror, expectant with fear, not knowing what he would find. "Doyle," he yelled, "Hildreth, get in here!"

Out the side door, he strode towards the swing set that sat shiny and new in the yard.

"Coming, Father, I'm sorry. I told Mommy all I remember. It's my fault, isn't it, Daddy?" Hildreth cowered as she reached her father.

"No, child, I'm not mad at you. I need to know where your brother is." Larry held Hildreth's shoulder in his big, strong hand. "Do you know where he is?"

Hildreth looked down at the ground, shaking her head.

* * *

The days that followed were filled as much with desperation as hate…at the circumstances…at the world…hoping for God's grace to show a morsel of reprise. Searches were undertaken, questions asked. The focus was on what needed to get done to find their only son. But with each knock at the door, Larry and Gladys' hopes dwindled.

One week and three days later, the answer came. *Ring, ring, ring…* Larry turned to Gladys, who no longer sprang to respond to the wooden box on the wall in hopes that it might offer good news. Instead, she trembled as she walked into the kitchen in slow motion. Somehow she knew that this call would be different.

"Yes, hello."

"Mrs. Falkner, this is Sheriff Lancaster," the voice said quietly, almost tenderly. "Can you and your husband come down to the hospital, please? I'm afraid I have bad news. I need you to corroborate that in fact we have found your son." The Sheriff knew his words were stabbing his neighbor in the heart. "I am so sorry, Gladys."

Only silence echoed the horror.

"Gladys, are you there? Hello?"

The chime of death had rung. Larry looked at Gladys and knew. They did not speak; they didn't have to. The trip was made, trudged through with silent despair. Arrangements settled.

* * *

Ironically, Doyle's body had been found at the same rail yard where Larry worked. The police spent weeks trying to find the killer who had brought such filth and hatred to the small town. Never again did Larry work; although he was told his job would always be there, he never returned. Instead, the bottle became Larry's friend. As he stumbled to the couch in the middle of the night for months on end, the four hideous horsemen slept by his side. Local investigators finally did figure out who killed their son: Charles Mercer was the vagrant's name, a carnival bum. They traced his path to an abandoned warehouse in Union. The local press called him the "Child Murderer." But by then it was too late.

The trial was short and without surprise; they convicted Mercer to life in prison. Some would say that was too good for a human who had left no mark on this earth except to kill and pillage. Others said a torturous death would make God's world complete. Either way, no solution would reclaim the soul of Larry's only son and fill the void left behind. In light of all the ugliness, no one was surprised at Larry's suicide, which followed shortly after.

Even though history cannot recount the terror of such a tragedy on these mortal victims, the damage is easily recognized. Damage of spirit; the lack of trust; locking the door at night for fear of the unseen... All who came after would carry the weight, paying a toll for passage to the next generation.

* * *

Sound travels far inside a home at night for every child who hears the whispers and tears through the upstairs banister. Just as this ripple in one family's history grew to a wave of fear, so did the stature of the individuals who had witnessed it. The future carries the scars from the harm done before. One hopes that the past will allow us to shape and control the next step, to avoid the dangers, the foolish errors and mistakes that echo the last generation, and the one before that. But instead, the path, though inviting with its colors of gold and silver and the sounds of laughter and joy, is also shrouded in mystery, obscured in grays. Never in our silent moments of illusion do we sense the dark parallel that lives beside us. Nor do we suspect the carrier.

Chapter 2

RESTRAINT

The years went by. The Parker family grew, healthy and with great promise. The '29 fall had come and gone with little affect on their close network of caring members. That fate was not shared by many others, however, and times were tough for those less fortunate.

It was now 1932. Jobs became available again to most who wanted them and, as with all misfortune, so came great opportunity. By trade, Robert Parker was a builder and he had made sure all his children knew how to work with their hands in order to provide. The lone girl, Martha used the skills she learned as well, taking care of the interior of the house. The Parkers were a great team and soon the boys were working closely with their father. The oldest, Bill, was the first to sign on to serve his country; the rest followed close behind. The service made a man out of you, and everyone said it was the right thing to do—perhaps the only thing. With the right nod from your parents, a strong young man could join at sixteen without any trouble. In fact, it was a great honor.

Indiana summers offered a collection of challenges and avenues for teenagers too young to join the military. Sharing in the work of the family business or helping with farming chores put a little pocket money in what was otherwise a poor existence. When the fair came to town, life became brighter, exciting… Suddenly lives which had been dull and predictable were bursting with possibility. Whole families came to ride the rides and enjoy the long summer nights under the colored lights. The sound of bells, laughter, and screams and the taste of caramel, sugarcane, and root beer filled the air for miles. On this particular summer night Hildy, as she preferred to be called these days, and the boys walked down the Midway in unison.

"Hey, Johnny, I bet you can't knock those balls down this year," goaded Tom.

"Can too! You just wait, I'll show you," Johnny said.

Benny and the others laughed. Hildy walked alongside Johnny, her curly hair bouncing. She gave him a big nudge. "I know you can knock them down, Johnny. I believe you," she said.

"Thanks, Hildy. You're always in my corner, aren't you?"

Hildy grabbed Johnny's hand and they ran off into the sea of people to become lost in the dusky lights.

"I bet they don't come back for a while," Jack said.

"They better be careful and not let father find them together again," said Benny.

The boys smirked and turned to pay closer attention to the group of roughnecks heading their way. Not a word was spoken, but a glossary of facial wars was playing out on their faces. The two clans of children squared off, readying for battle. The distance between them closed and then closed some more. Just as it shrunk to nil, the air thick with tension.

At the last moment, all eyes focused on the ground at their feet and they passed each other by.

It was a victory of sorts, and great sighs of relief were released.

"Who was that? Did they know you?" Benny asked Jack.

"Yeah, I know them. Those were the Carter boys from the other side of town. Their dad has that tool shop so they think they're slick and tough." Jack spoke with resentment and frustration. "That big one, his name's Donny. Watch out for him, he'll cut cha to look atcha."

In a town of so few, names and faces are known to all and not much is left to secret. An advantage to the privileged few; a burden of proof to the masses.

* * *

"Johnny, why do they say that our kissing is forbidden when it feels so right?"

The two figures were shadowed in the light against the side of the barn. Wrapped in a warm embrace, they talked of lover's dreams.

"Well, we're cousins and all," Johnny answered, his voice full of confusion. "They say you ain't supposed to, 'cause of God and all, I guess. But Hildy, if'n I was gonna marry someone, I sure hope they're just like you."

"You think we could ever have kids, John? I want lots of kids, and they say we shouldn't do that either. Can we anyway...please? You know I love you more than anyone else in the world..."

At the tender ages of seventeen and fourteen, Johnny and Hildreth knew that folks got married and started families all the time. But they were also old enough to know that the sin of incest was just that—a sin.

There was nothing that explained the attraction between them, not the closeness of the two families or the loss of Hildreth's brother. But the more their families tried to tear them apart, the more Johnny and Hildreth sought to connect. The families mutely agreed to deny what was in front

17

of them as long as they could. It was only when it became obvious that nothing they could do would change the outcome that the families accepted, albeit in quiet disgust, the situation. Embarrassed over Hildy's "status" and the upcoming nuptials, the Parkers agreed a simple ceremony with a justice of the peace would be best.

Robert made it clear to Johnny that he was to work hard and become his apprentice. Hildy's pregnancy ensured John would work extra hard and Robert made sure of it. John's duty to war and country was side-stepped, as his brothers and even his sister went to join their big brother Bill in the Army. Although Johnny had always had a reputation as the class clown and the joker of the family, nobody was smiling over the times ahead. They knew that even if birth defects avoided the family now, they would likely eventually manifest in future generations.

Silently, with fear in their hearts, they agreed to stay mute. If the children from this union were healthy and safe, they would be better off not speaking of it again. After all, pride and distinction were important. Further disclosure would only destroy something that had become so strong in recent years. And that was not going to happen on Robert Parker's watch!

Mary stayed close to her sister Gladys until her death. Some say her broken heart took her sooner than she should have gone. Either way, Mary felt a moral duty to care for Hildy when Gladys passed away. Devastated but dedicated, Mary continued to stand by her children as Hildy and John's life unfolded. Her faith was strong, but she blamed herself for not seeing the signs early enough, or perhaps for not doing something to prevent them from becoming so dependent on one another. Not knowing the answer drove Mary to religious worship, hoping for a better, everlasting eternity for sinners. In essence, Mary became the matriarch for this ship of fools.

* * *

Whether by silence or sin by omission, each who willingly goes this way will pass the corpses of those whom he hurts. I believe that each sin carries a value and that its cost holds a judgment in purgatory. Although everything that occurred and everything that was to follow may not be clearly understood by those of us in life, we must always ask the questions. It matters not that we assign ourselves a religious persuasion; it matters not where we spend our final days. Though this may be something we cannot accept until we accept the inevitability of our own death, what matters is that we leave the way we came into this world, with God by our side.

Chapter 3

MIDWAY THROUGH…

It was 1939. As the newly formed Parker family grew with the last of three (first Charlie, then Charlotte, and now Norma Jean) born, happiness was everywhere. With their family healthy and happy (except for Hildreth's sugar problem), Robert's dream for and ideals of a safe generation to follow had come true. By now, Johnny had become a well-known builder and construction supervisor for his Dad and was looking at other opportunities to further his family's legacy.

The children became strong; their generation showed character and held onto the principles handed down by a family that had risen from constraints. The men came home safely from battle, strengthened by combat. Pride in America and the new opportunities presented provided hope and direction for everyone. The Parkers stayed close as a family unit, coming together at heartfelt family reunions. Robert had begun to slow down this year, 1949, and the duty of gathering the family fell to John. It was summer again and the fair was once more in town. Cars lined the drive of the family home, on display. Children bounced and played, watchful eyes following every move. Laughter and food was plentiful, cold beer and good conversation adding to the joyful occasion. Family came from as far as California, where Tommy and Martha had settled after the war. All agreed it was a great time to be alive.

As dusk began to set on the events of the day, the older children, including Charlie and his sisters, Janet, and Rocky—there must have been ten of them altogether—decided to go to the fair. With sheepish grins and polite respect they asked to go and were told yes, as long as each was responsible for the group and nobody was left alone. Excited, they advanced down the drive to walk the mile or so to the fair gates. Their walk took them over the railroad tracks that lined the middle of the road deep inside the shadows of town.

Here in this town the tracks that once haunted the family still brought on a moment of fear, one of doubt and confusion of the kind that flashes across one's mind. In that flash of clarity, one finds oneself experiencing either a moment of relief—or of confinement. It was no different for these children except that they knew on which side of the tracks they belonged, and had the comfort of knowing they would return to a place of security and love.

"Hey, who's that?" Charlie said.

Down the edge of the dirty road that followed the tracks into darkness stood two figures partly in shadow, a man and a boy, by the looks of them. Caught by the raised voices, the group paused and watched the scene unfold.

"Go to hell, you sonofabitch. You're a filthy drunk. All you do is hurt us! I wish you would just go away!" the boy's voice carried from the shadows.

They heard a door slam, loud enough to shake the hinges that held it. "Go to hell, punk, leave me alone," the man yelled.

Then there was a violent burst, the sound of a muffler exploding, as if in anger. Dust flew up and around the truck, which was suddenly barreling toward the children, driven insanely. It lurched by the group, only to stop

as aggressively as it had started next to a building down the street. The

sign above the door read "Sam's Place." A large jagged man emerged to

disappear inside the bar, and likely inside the bottle. The evil of hard

liquor was clearly the winner of this battle. The fact is that this side of the

tracks offered only more of the same: confinement to your own personally

defined hell. The children recognized the same evil in what they witnessed

that had given rise to the stories about their great uncle. Today, their

distance from a slice of reality was just enough to keep them safe from

something they knew, that life was frail and layered with dark avenues of

change.

Later that evening, the girls among them veered off a little ways and

left the boys to etch out their egos. They soon came across another group

of young men. This year at the fair was no different from others, of course,

the children and young adults gathering, declaring their territories. Though

more alike than different, each group still wanted to carve out a unique

identity it could call its own. As the block of boys came towards them, giggling laughter was instantly replaced by shy, reserved postures and they huddled instinctively. The young women, feeling the shift, stopped and huddled too. There was safety in numbers.

"Don't say anything, now, you don't know these boys!" Janet said to the group.

"I'll talk if I want to!" returned Charlotte, a stocky, determined teenager.

"You keep your mouth shut, you're going to get us in trouble!" Norma hissed.

"Trouble, why, that's my middle name," said a boy, interrupting. "Who wants to know what my first name is?" Standing tall with iced hair, in a pair of jeans that hovered above white socks, Billy's black shoes reflected colors from their Saturday-night shine. "It's Billy."

"Never mind my brother there," said another. "He doesn't know how to talk to a fine girl like yourself." The shorter but more confident young man looked at Norma Jean as he spoke. "But I sure would like to try. They call me Johnny."

Demur yet forward for a young woman of her upbringing, Norma was quick to recognize the attention. She turned away, but with a glimpse of a smile to let Johnny know she accepted his advance. Meanwhile, Charlotte was busy being playing the mouse in a game of excitement. Hormones, hours of preparation to dress and to sculpt the hair just so…all to ensure the door would be open to the chance that young love could enter—without parental knowledge. The anticipation crackled in the air like a game of catch without the need for a trap.

After a while, the thrill of forbidden fruit wore off enough that the clans went their separate ways, having noted the others and now having the fodder for great gossip for the rest of the night. As the sounds began to quiet and the dirt began to show on everyone's shoes, winnings were collected, losses lamented, and the group walked home. Some walked in pairs, others alone, but they were never out of each other's sight, especially when crossing to the other side of the tracks, something they always did in unison.

Another night at the fair was over.

* * *

Is it in that brief moment referenced in hindsight when we notice our lives are connected? Some might say it's divine intervention or spirituality that should take credit. Can such questions ever be answered? Can there be complete agreement before time ends? I don't think so, at least based on what little I may have to offer. But I can tell you that forming judgment before investigation is a continuing theme throughout the rest of this story. What parallel events are in our lives today? What experiences have we had that have altered or denied others? Can we predict or expect good or evil? Should we? As this story unfolds, you will read how my life has been filled with episodes of déjà vu and glimpses of reality clouded by time and the tales of others. There is remorse and regret over actions taken, or sometimes not taken, the acceptance of or credit for tasks traced back to a time remembered through a veil. It would seem the thing we search for in life might well be right next to us, but often we are so consumed with the future solution to our plight that we overlook the obvious links to the present. A scholar I am not. In fact, I take on this story only to leave a trace of my participation and interpretation as a bow to a larger purpose. Simply, I feel compelled to identify that which makes me human and allows me to exist...all there is that provides proof that I was here.

Life was full for the Parker family. It was 1957 and the girls were coming into their own. John, also called J. P. or Pap by some, was proud and rightfully so of the life he'd built, supporting his family and being able to offer them many chances for education and travel. Since their last visit to the fair the summer before, Charlotte had become a seamstress, and had gone to work for Singer as a garment worker, Charlie had joined the Navy, and Norma was getting ready to graduate high school. Norma's desire for a modeling or acting career had faded, but she was still a shining star. The year before, for her birthday, she'd been given the gift of a full portrait, professionally painted, to use to pursue a modeling career. Norma had become a woman, a beautiful woman, who learned early on that her grace and education, combined with God's gift of beauty, would take her far. Her inner beauty did not take a distant second either, as light radiated from every corner of her being.

The tall skinny young man from the fair, the one named Billy, was calling on Charlotte. But Johnny had set his sights on a prize way outside his reach when he set them on Norma. Not the types to give up easily, the boys had a plan to remove them from the life they lived on the other side of town. Frankly, social divides were common in this town in those times.

Johnny, whose heart, compassion, and drive to better his life were matched only by the fear of failure and the loneliness that came with the rejection of those watching from across the tracks, did not give up.

J. P. bought some land and began building a new home for the family. Land was still innocent then and Indiana cornfields lined the view for miles. With Charlie gone, the need for help was constant, but if there were to be ties between Billy, Johnny and the two Parker women, it would have to go through J. P. first. To court a man's daughter, one's intent and implementation was critical. In this case, one daughter experienced only a modicum of oversight; the other was under lock and key. Nobody got close to Norma without J. P.'s knowledge and approval. But it didn't take long before Johnny and Norma were falling in love. Norma was the prettiest girl in school and Johnny, the leatherneck, wielded an image to defend.

Soon Norma, fifteen, and Johnny, twenty, could regularly be found in the malt shop after class. Admiration or fascination, who could say, but their eyes and hearts connected. Norma was the envy of all as she rode in Johnny's car, a rat rod that could win a race without spilling a drop of gas. Johnny resembled that little-known Cutter from Fairmont, James Dean. Life was easy.

On most Saturday nights, the crowd could be found either at the drive-in or cruising Madison and Main, the streets that ran the length of the town and offered a great place to race—if you didn't get caught! On this night, as they sat in the car under the light of the movie screen at the drive-in, Johnny would tell Norma something that would alter their lives forever.

"What has you so quiet tonight, Johnny? Is something wrong?" Norma asked.

After a pause, Johnny said, "I have to leave soon. I've signed up for the Marines!" His voice was full of pride, but when he saw Norma's face, it got muffled. "I didn't know how to tell you, so this is it. I wish I knew a better way, Norma, but the good news is when I get done with boot camp, maybe you could come with me." Excited again, Johnny continued. "I can get us a house and we can move to California and live in the sunshine, go to the beach, play in …"

"STOP! how could you?" Norma screamed. Her tears spilled over. "John Ronald! You told me you would stay here! …Work with Father, learn a trade, and care for us! Why, why now? Take me home!"

Not another word was spoken on the trip back. The rumble of exhaust slowly hushed as they pulled in front of J. P.'s. Without turning, Norma opened the door and got out.

"Can I call you later?" John asked weakly.

Norma paused and bent down to the window, "Why?" Norma walked away knowing this was the last time she would see Johnny, perhaps for forever.

A week later, Johnny left for the Marines. The town never even noticed he was gone. The two lovers never spoke again in person. A few weeks went by, and his letters piled up at the Parker family home. Hildreth began keeping the patriotic red and blue-striped envelopes inside the never-opened drawer by the front door. Hildreth struggled with what the right thing to do was, hoping Norma was not aware of their existence, and after a month or so they stopped. The life of the brokenhearted teenager continued, perhaps a little less bright, but hopefully stronger for the effort.

Meanwhile, the Parker family went about its affairs. Over time, many individuals would make their way to the door, including an older man with whom Charlotte formed a relationship, a man who would prove to be abusive to her. In a town small with intimate tales of struggle and strife, knowledge travels quickly. But it served no use for J. P. to try to intervene because Charlotte's strong will and determination would hear no reason.

Soon she was pregnant, so the only option was unhappy acceptance of the situation. The child would be born, a frightening reality because Charlotte was fragile and weak already. And with the stress of the pregnancy, the emotional turmoil was beginning to have an effect.

The result was a rollercoaster of emotional and physical outbursts that often led to emergency room visits. Unfortunately, this would become a pattern in Charlotte's life that never changed. Eight months pregnant on a cold February night with a wind that could cut a leg off from the chill and all the family present, Charlotte lay in a hospital bed in fear of losing her child. In 1958, nobody made the connection between diabetes and its effects on pregnancy.

"The child will die if we do not take it now," said the doctor, in a white jacket and glasses. "Can you protect the child without hurting Charlotte?" the family wanted to know.

"Yes," he said, "but the time is now. The child is our second concern; she is our first."

Hildreth and J. P. stood firm, short in stature but with a presence that always demanded attention. "Then you need to make that happen!" J. P. growled. Hildreth nodded in agreement.

The white coat disappeared around the corner. Prayers of faith were said that both mother and child would be healthy.

The absence of Charlotte's husband was obvious to all present, although nothing was said. About an hour passed before the man in the white coat returned, this time his approach less pronounced and slower in stride. "I have some good news," he said, "you have a baby girl. But there are some complications." At that moment words of anger, thoughts of incest, forbidden love, hate, evil, wrong, freaks, and all that is taboo came flooding into the hearts and minds of the little group in the waiting room. Hildreth began to weep. She fell into a hard seat, gasping for her next breath. "Is it Charlotte or the baby?"

The doctor replied, "It's the baby. Although she is fully developed, it appears that she may have a clubfoot, a deformity that will require correction. Now, don't get me wrong, the child is in no danger. In fact, she is doing wonderfully, as is the mother."

Through the shame, nobody could hear the doctor's optimism.

The family spent the rest of the evening comforting Charlotte. Arrangements were made to take care of the baby in short order. Not being a family to ignore the truth of what was before them, they all rallied. It could have been worse.

* * *

Time went on, winter replaced by spring in full bloom. The baby was named Jenny. The doctors had preformed minor surgery and constructed a corrective brace that helped straighten Jenny's legs.

The man in Charlotte's life had successfully avoided playing any part in his daughter's birth or life. Nobody knew much about him either. But then the bad news came. No sooner had she been advised that another child would be a mistake, Charlotte was quick to announce a second would be born in another eight months. The news rested heavily on the hearts and consciences of the family members. But what were they to do?

J. P. and Hildy led a life both successful and stable. They were comfortable in their role as patriarch and matriarch and as grandparents. But fabricated environments can only hold up for so long when they are built on sand. Their secret and forbidden union had begun to reveal damaging effects on innocent participants of the next generation.

Chapter 4

STRANGERS MEET

The summer sun was bravely harsh in August, 1958, burning the skin, searing the paint of a house, leaving nothing unseen and no place to hide. It seems life has a way of punishing some and this season was no exception. Charlotte spent her days hard at work, both delighted and apprehensive at the idea that she would soon be having another baby. Chores became harder and harder as she suffered from physical pain and heat exhaustion. The father of her children had vanished again. An unwed woman, labeled and tarnished as "mentally challenged," raising a child and expecting another, Charlotte reached every day for the faith to believe that God's world had purpose. Her diligent attendance at the local church kept her grounded and her family's support held her together.

This year the county fair returned as usual, but circumstances were not the same. With graduation came the responsibility for finding work and defining the future. I suppose this challenge comes to everyone and this was the year for Norma. In high school, Norma excelled in accounting and typing. Therefore, it only seemed natural for her to take a job at the local drugstore, helping in the office, keeping records, and caring for the store. A good job for a fine young lady, you might say. The young woman who walked the boardwalk was tired after a day at work, but eager to gaze at the night lights and enjoy the Midway. Today was a special event, the demolition derby.

"Pardon me, Mr. Dalton, do you mind if I take off a little early today?" Norma asked her boss timidly, her green eyes dancing. "Say around four o'clock? It's the fair and all and Cathy and I want to go."

"Ugh-hm." The stout, well-dressed man cleared his throat and Norma held her breath. Would he refuse her request?

"I assume you will be making up the time you miss, Norma, is that correct?" Mr. Dalton said sternly.

"Oh, of course, sir," said Norma.

Mr. Dalton nodded and Norma thanked him graciously and then went off to attend to her last duties before quitting time.

When Norma got home, J. P. announced that he had just returned from a trip down south where he had found some real estate he wanted to buy. Hildreth, reserved by nature, was quick to ask all the right questions, hoping to keep her husband from making what could be a man-sized mistake.

"Now, now, Hildy, you need to see this place before you scold me," J. P. said. "I was driving home, saw a sign and stopped. The man wants a fair dollar! I believe we can finally build that home in the woods we've always wanted."

"Well, if you think it's best, J. P.," said Hildy. "I admit you haven't gone wrong yet."

And so J. P. purchased over forty acres of prime raw woodlands on the crest of a mountain in Brown County with the name of Trail's End. In deep winter in this neck of the woods, the leaves fold away their coats of scarlet red and gold to let the chill of winter blanket the ground with ice and snow. The wind is loud and strong, though the dogwoods and the oaks stand firm. Every sound echoes loudly as it travels across the surface of the snow. Those who live in the area call it Gnaw-bone and no wonder, because with each trip to the outhouse, the chill was quick to do exactly that. But somehow, the residents of this paradise did not mind paying the price.

When J. P. and Hildy stood in the shadow of tall tress, looking out at their land, it was clear this spot would become home. Serenity touched their souls, and they felt grateful. The joy of family reunions and happiness was surely not far behind. In the spring creatures and sights, and an escape from the everyday world, would be theirs. The restless nights were filled with anticipation, minds busy with planning and purpose. It was going to be grand, as J. P. said, simply grand.

* * *

Back in town, the sun had long set. The sounds of the fair echoed for miles. The girls walked through the streets of this small town as they had for years. This year was different, though, because the girls had become women whose grace had emerged and now accompanied each step they took. They walked with that particular sway, the one of confident women everywhere.

"So, are you going to talk to him tonight?" Cathy asked.

"Talk to whom?" Norma asked, putting just the right amount of boredom into her voice.

"Oh, you don't fool me, Norma, so don't you play that game. Donny, of course! You know he'll be here tonight. Butch said that we could double date on the Ferris wheel, if you want."

"I don't know if Donny is my type, Cathy. He's handsome, but his family scares me, especially his dad. His mom is real nice, though."

Soon the young women had reached the fair's main gate, where the smell of cotton candy and root beer met their noses and the sound of the barkers, enticing the crowd to join the festivities, rung in the air.

The young man at the fair stood away from the crowd for a moment to observe. Life has a way of slowing down and then hastening on without our noticing sometimes; this time and place was no different. The boy this young man had been, the one who had stood boldly in the dim light of the railroad tracks and who had found his future defined in that moment, was the same man who now held tightly to the stature of the adult he had become. His father had long since gone, taking the boy's childhood with him before his thirteenth birthday. The boy's mother, Velma, was a broken woman, forced to become dependent on her only son, Donny.

Four generation

Velma's mother, Flossie, was the family matriarch and provided deep roots of stability for an otherwise unstable family unit. Tales of Don Sr.'s drunken rampages could be heard through the town's gossip mills, only to be swept quietly aside by Flossie and her husband, Fred. In this small town where the automobile was king, you either built cars or houses. If you did neither, you made sure you went to church, where you tried to

gain sanity, or at least legitimacy, through your faith in God. If that didn't

work, and your soul was left to wallow in mental, emotional, and spiritual

bankruptcy, you drank yourself into oblivion. But whatever you decided,

the town knew about it. Most of the performing functioning fools would

tell you they were great chaps when sober and Don Sr. was no different. A

toolmaker by trade, Don might have made a great living for his family. As

it was, it only created a great opportunity to be a drunkard.

Standing six foot five or better, Donny's dad was only a couple inches

taller than Donny. Through the years Donny heard about his father's antics

from his grandmother. He knew that Don Sr, when sober, was the best

toolmaker around, but when drunk he'd often end in Detroit and need to

be flown back to town to face relentless shame each and every time.

Flossie was haunted by her devotion to do what was right, her love for her

daughter and grandson overpowering any social curse she had to endure. It

was her daughter's life at stake, after all, which meant no price was too

high to pay.

Donald Jr. was to follow in his father's occupational footsteps and without complaint he too went to work for the same company, Product Tool. He seemed to have a knack for the work. Supported by his grandfather Fred, who also worked there, the fit was tight and snug—as were the secrets that would follow. For now, though, the waves were relatively soft, at least on the days the ship was right. Donny had taken on the task of caring for his mother. His chore was simple: to care for the most important person in the world. Donny never was a complainer, even with his inner rage about the past. He focused instead on his vision of the better life he was sure would appear.

Donny arrived at the fair with his friends, Charlie and Butch. Don was tall and well-groomed, a powerful example of a hardworking nineteen-year-old full of testosterone. Butch, the smallest of the group, was something of a cut-up, a scrappy, feisty character, good to have around whenever you needed a laugh or a bright idea. Charlie was as honest as they come, his place in the group only challenged when someone else got it in his head to join their small click. In blood and brotherhood, however, this gang of comrades stood strong. Donny had heard about Norma's sister and about Norma's own fling with the Norris family, and the knowing gave Norma an aura of excitement and intrigue. Tonight Don was going to find out what was so special about this young woman.

"Butch, you'd better not set me up with a horse, I'll smack you into next week." Don said in a smoke-tarred voice.

"Geez, Donny, give me some slack, man. I wouldn't do you that way. Besides if Cathy is her best friend, you think she's going to be any less of a doll?"

Laughing, Charlie was quick to point out the last time Butch pulled a prank on the gang, "If you do, Butch, I'd make sure to run real far after that last hoax you pulled. You almost got us all killed by that gal's old man."

"Damn right, that was a close one," Donny said, slapping Charlie on the back.

"Hey, Chuck," Don said more softly, "thanks for helping Mom with her groceries. I appreciate that. She has a rough time of it, but she always tells me how you help her. You're the best, pal." Charlie humbly shook his head, embarrassed. He'd only done what was the right thing to do for his "family."

"Hey, you." Butch gave a loud whistle and signaled to the women walking in the gate, "Over here."

With one leg on a bench, cigarette in hand, Donny abruptly stood at attention. He tossed aside the butt, brushed off his black leather jacket, and made a quick brush of his hair by his hand against the perfectly formed coal black silk. His legs presented a pressed line in the crease of his jeans, and his physique revealed the instant icon of a proud young man.

Charlie glanced over and whispered, "She looks like a keeper, Donny. Don't screw this one up, chump."

"Where you girls been, we've been waiting for a half hour. Hey, Norma, this here is Donald Carter, we call him Donny. You know Charlie."

"Hi," said the young women together.

"I've heard a lot about you, Mr. Carter," Norma said. "Are you the rough guy everyone says you are? Cathy told me to watch out for you," Norma's eyes let everyone know she was joking.

"Well, I think I can carry my own. But I know how to treat a fine lady, too!"

It was at that moment that the world went silent.

Some say it was love at first sight; others say the chase began. A student of religion might tell you that God, the crowning Creator, stepped in to reveal two people's divine path. Others might argue that divinity is nothing more than a collection of exaggerated emotions explained by science and that in this world we should only believe what we can see or touch. But at this moment, two parallel universes collided.

Parallel: always the same distance apart and therefore never meeting, like two voices singing together but preserving the same pitch intervals all the way along. Only this melody suddenly met and the pitch coincided with a jolt as Norma's eyes met Donny's. And suddenly Donny could think of nothing else but winning the prize, the heart of the beautiful woman who had captured his full attention.

The night flew by in flashes of exhibitionism, blatant femininity, and naïve laughter. The bonds formed would last a lifetime, but what was to follow would strain the patience of any man or woman. Questions would be asked that no reason could answer. Homes would be destroyed, souls burned. All eyes would strain to focus on a phoenix that might raise their spirits. If only they could have seen or known…but perhaps they did. Perhaps in the seeing they chose not to acknowledge what they saw. Perhaps they would come to regret their actions, to have remorse for what they were to do. In the amber cast of light across the dirt Midway, however, on this summer night at the fair, two innocent lives came together, orchestrated somehow, to play out a scene only rehearsed many times before; to embark on a journey that began at its fullest, full of encouragement and hope. Still young enough to shed any inconvenient thought of damp, unwelcome sorrows, the men and women of this small town were ready to take on the world.

This year the fair provided solace, comfort in its fantasy, illusion, and grandeur. The barkers, roadies, and drifters huddled together, counting their rewards with tales of thieving, each one with a taller story than the last. The smell of livestock, considered gold by some, left a path of dust and dirt, tired children at their heels to catch loose stragglers. But everyone came of one mind and left different, altered, in ways they could not always recognize. Prizes won, heartaches matched by stomach pains, all with a cost—but worth the effort, according to those who had them. Moms and dads let their innocent offspring believe that they too could reach for the golden ring, that perhaps there was more to this world then what had been provided. In the end, was it truth or fantasy?

How was one to know if he or she were being led down the right path? The fair gave hope in its abundance of adrenalin and excitement, the sense that anyone could knock down the pins and lay down his burdens, no matter how heavy. Surely, this collection of souls had paid their dues and tolls so they would have access to enjoy the fruit of God's world.

Chapter 5

WEDDING DAY

October 1958 was brisk, interrupted only by a short, sweet Indian summer, after which the colors fell swiftly to the ground with abandon. A blanket of sage, sienna, ocher, orange, and yellow covered the town. Random specs of white and gray buildings offered a checkerboard appeal. This was the view today from the church down the way, but most were not aware for the flurry of activity in their midst. Today was the wedding day!

Tucked away in the back of the church a gaggle of ladies could be found scurrying to find the right shoes, the right hats, the right gloves, all frenzied with anticipation. Though the pace was frantic, the anxiety high, each lady was poised, lovely in her exuberance. The aisles of the church were covered in flowers of garnet and yards of matching fabric. The sun was warm, rays of light poking their way through the windows, heightening each glistening sparkle of color. The men too were busy, splashing water in their eyes, shaving away the bachelor party from the night before. Laughter was everywhere—with one interruption. Unfortunately, the groom's father had decided to present himself at the event. Since today was not the time or place for either the admittance of an uncomfortable reality or the disclosure of secrets, it was silently agreed that all present would hold their tongues.

"Cathy! Where's my makeup bag?" shouted a partially dressed bride.

"Here, right next to you, Norma. Jeez, you think Donny can hear you?"

"Settle down, my dear, this too shall pass." Norma's mother had appeared to allay all fears and concerns, though her own lay just under the surface. "This fretting will get you nowhere. Your father and I are proud and pleased for you."

Charlotte spoke up as well. "Sis, you're going to be fine. Just remember we all love you dearly and God will watch over you and your new family forever."

Norma was excited, but confused as well about what to do with this feeling she was experiencing. "Can you gals leave for just a second, please? I need to talk to Mom. You too, Sis."

Perhaps a bit offended, the others left politely. The door slowly closed and Norma began to weep. "Mom, I haven't told Donny about our family history and I'm afraid. What if he finds out and leaves—like his dad did?" Norma's voice trembled with anxiety. "I could not live through a divorce. It wouldn't be right, it would be shameful. Please tell me what to do, should I still marry him or tell him now?"

Norma's mascara had begun to streak. Her mother wiped the dark smears with a tissue and said, "Norma Jean, you need to understand that these are your choices. I cannot make them for you. If this man loves you and your life together is to be, then any news you share now or later is only going to make you stronger. J. P. and I have struggled with this. You know we are not ones to judge…we have our own failings. Nevertheless, you and our family together are blessed. Follow your heart, dear, you will make the right choice."

"But what if something happens? You know, like Sissy's girl. I don't know if I can do that."

A soft knock at the door silenced the women and light entered the room. The figure at in the doorway stood as if readied for battle, and then entered the room with purpose. "What's wrong, child, today is your day," the tall confident woman said.

"Hello, Flossie, Norma just has the jitters," said Hildreth.

"Well, I can tell you this, today is your wedding and you're the star! You don't think I made these gowns up for nothing," Flossie jested.

The ladies laughed and soon fears, replaced by the usual pre-wedding nerves, had been all but forgotten. The room filled once again with chatter and laughter. The players were ready to follow the script set before them.

As the grand array of pews filled with family and friends, never was a place so alive. It seemed that the chain of despair which had held tight to the Carter family had finally been broken. Surely something this glorious could do no wrong.

Butch and Cathy stood by as Norma and Donald became one that day. Filled with the anticipation of his and their potential, Don Jr. was sure he would not repeat the past. It was his intent to protect this woman until the day they would part in death, God help him. Norma, too, felt the need to set the past aside and honor her heritage.

"I now proudly introduce Mr. and Mrs. Donald Carter," said the pastor, and it was done. If ever this town of strangers would witness a storybook tale, this was the one.

Their apartment was conveniently located above Flossie and Fred's home and the couple quickly settled in. In the meantime, Butch and Cathy made their own announcement to wed and soon the cast had reassembled for their nuptials. It was a year of celebration and good days for certain, and everyone reveled in the festivities. Weekly card parties and other gatherings further cemented the bond between friends. One day Flossie appeared at Donnie's job with the unhappy news that his mother had passed away. Velma had been sick for years, never rallying after so much heartache. One might have expected Donny to be angry but he only became quietly somber. His new wife alone was able to provide solace and comfort. His grandmother Flossie understood. Ever since his father had left, Donny had not been able to be a child. Now, at nineteen, the man had become an orphan. Distant relatives abounded in Indianapolis and were quick to offer condolences, but Don trusted only one direction—inward—and the one person who would never desert him—himself.

It had become Don and Norma Jean's tradition to celebrate New Year's Eve with Butch and Cathy. This year the holiday came a few months after Velma's passing and several other weddings. Don and Norma went off to pick up Butch, Cathy, Charlie, and his new bride Mona, and another couple they'd met recently at Field House. They piled into Don's shiny car. Norma and her handsome husband had eagerly engaged in a march up the ladder into middle-class America and loved to show it off. With touches of premature gray appearing at the edge of his temples, Don was a respected, prominent man for his age. Not to mention that his wife could stop a bus with her looks, given half a chance.

"Watch your shoes everyone, or I'll put you in the trunk," Don said with a hint of seriousness. "He's the only one who can fit," Charlie laughed and pointed to Butch.

Laughter and giggling ensued and the car, a beautiful, slightly used 1957 pink Cadillac, took off.

The night was overflowing with the spirit of joy in the glittering, smoke-filled room. The sultry air and musky perfumes teased even the most honest of men who challenged the battlefield for the catch of the night, knowing the manner of this chase was important because it was said that "ladies walk slower, but women stand still." Norma and Don spent the night in an embrace, captured by the atmosphere. The couples enjoyed a carefree night, setting inhibitions aside with courage and loud voices and the expectation of a new virgin life to be rung in with the dawn.

* * *

I've been told that the future is not of our own making, that fate may have a far greater impact than planning or preparation. Some would be quick to say that all is divine and that once a direction is set, it cannot be altered. I believe, as do the characters in this story, that nothing happens in God's world by mistake. A carryover from the lessons of my elders, perhaps, but I believe it takes more than good intentions to change the course of a life. In fact, I would say that sometimes our own actions are in conflict with the beliefs we hold so tightly.

The time for second-guessing is now gone, however. So let be it known to the players involved that a new day and a new life had started, its precipice inviting them to lean over the edge with faith. It is that faith that will define the way Norma and Don perceive the world, and will shift their awareness forever.

Chapter 6

LONG HOT SUMMER; SHORT STORY

Spring arrived early that year and the smell of fragrant flowers permeated the sheets on the line and carried across the windowsills. Living on the second floor allowed the breeze to flow and dance inside the small apartment that would quickly be outgrown by its inhabitants. On this April day, Flossie had come to check the icebox, adjust the curtains, hem a few pants, and of course offer a bit of advice or good judgment. As with most families, polite visits and reasonable guidance was always welcome, and today was no different.

"How are you feeling today, honey? Do you want me to bring your laundry up for you?" asked Flossie, coming over to sit by Norma, who was holding her round belly.

"Not necessary, Grandma, but it would be nice. I have just about hit my limit with chores. It's just so hot today! That fan you gave us helps a little, but a cold cloth is about the only thing that works."

Frail as Norma was, her body had taken on the new shape and delight of motherhood, but the strain of pregnancy it had put on her was painfully obvious as well. With Don's working so hard to earn money to pay for the new arrival, he had become more passive at home and absent more and more often. This would become a pattern for Donny, whether self-inflicted or as the consequence of his upbringing, no one knew. Norma, however, well aware of his reaction to her confession about her family's secret affairs and genealogical makeup, never challenged his involvement—or lack thereof. Providence had carved into the fabric of life what it had in store, as well as her part to play, and Norma prayed every day for guidance and delivery and to assuage the guilt she felt over the choices she had made.

The days were slow, the nights long. Each awakening brought an early departure by Don, who secured the door behind him. Today was no different, except for a flash of insight that let him know that today was the day his child would be born.

"I'll be here in a minute when you call, Norma. I just know today is the day that Kris will arrive." Donny was smiling and laughing as he sipped his morning coffee and got ready to leave.

Don had always said from the start that no matter what, boy or girl, the baby's name would be Kris and Norma agreed. Neither had focused on their fears of what the future would bring if they gave birth to a child with "problems." In fact, it had been just the opposite, and their aspirations could not have been higher.

"She'll be a beautiful girl, Norma, just like her mother!" said Don.

"And you get to change all the diapers," Norma kidded.

"Umm, yeah, sure…" Don gulped. "Whatever you say, Norma."

The two parted. Don walked down the stairs. He passed by the window of Flossie's house and waved good-bye. "Keep a close eye on her, and come and get me when it's time," he said. "I think today's the day, Grandma. Make sure the suitcase is in the car, too, please."

"I'm sure we'll be fine, Donny. Martha Rose said she was coming over later to help me jar up some berries. Norma will be careful. I was going to make some dinner tonight, if you'd like me to."

"Sure, Grandma. Thanks, you're the best."

"Love you, son, have a good day at work then."

It was already eighty degrees and the temperature and humidity were both climbing on this Labor Day, September 1, 1959. Restless and wanting to escape the heat upstairs, Norma went down to visit Flossie about an hour later. Flossie was quick to offer her a chair.

"Dear, dear, you are holding on to that baby, aren't you? You look exhausted, Norma, and the day hasn't even started, honey." No sooner had she spoken than a sheen of sweat appeared on Norma Jean's face. Seconds later, the rush of water could be heard splashing to the floor. Martha Rose had arrived moments before and together she and Flossie had the experience, knowledge, and wisdom to know just what to do.

Chapter 7

A CHILD ARRIVED

"BREATHE, breathe... Push!" Norma held tight to Flossie's hand, both for comfort and strength. J. P. sat in the corner, watching with tears in his eyes, of joy or pain it was hard to tell. Hildreth, Flossie, and Martha circled the bed. Don stood near the window, encouraging Norma at each push, his face flushed with worry and excitement. When Doctor Thomas walked into the room he was quick to ask the group to leave.

"Come along, Mother," said J. P., "it's time for the doctor. Let's go get a cup of coffee. Flossie, you two want to join us?" They left and shut the door.

Dr. Thomas quietly told the couple that he had great apprehension about the outcome of the moments to follow. He went on to say that he had taken the liberty to prepare a support team of nurses in case any "abnormalities" or "difficulties" arose. His meager assurances were of little comfort to the distressed couple.

"Is she going to be okay, Doctor?" Don turned away from Norma to speak to the doctor. He did not want to make Norma any more anxious than she already was.

"I have no real concerns for the health of the mother here. It's the child that needs our focus now. I am going to send in a nurse and we will prepare your wife for delivery. We are going to advance her labor shortly. I assume you will be in the room with us, Don?"

Don glanced at his wife. "Yes, of course," he said.

"Keep in mind, Don, Norma, that although our original review suggests there is potential for additional concern, we simply don't know. Don't forget, the good Lord above is in charge here, folks. We may have done all this worrying for just another normal, healthy baby. So let's keep that in mind."

Don and Norma heard the doctor's words, but little could quell their anxiety. In moments they would know the truth, the reality of what lay ahead. Would their child be a "normal, healthy" baby—or something else?

Delivery went smoothly and the mother was safe. But the sigh of relief that would certainly have followed was not to happen. One look, one split second was all it took to see that all was not as it should be in the mass of blood and fluids that had been expelled from Norma Jean's body. It seemed as if the clock stopped and the people attending in the room froze, knowing not what to say, not having the energy or courage to move from the spot.

The sounds of the hospital began to ring with an echo of detachment. The doctor's commands stumbled out in syllables until sentences grew into paragraphs that went unheard. The lights of the room brightened and the look on Don's face became violet with ire. God All Mighty himself had struck them with his wrath; he had sent down a terrifying lump of maleness, a deformed, distorted example of a human figure that resembled nothing as much as a sight of death. Surely, this thing was not human—or at least not the baby boy He would choose to produce! How could this be?

It took every ounce of medical training and experience for the doctor to summon the courage the circumstance demanded. Those still gasping with astonishment were asked to leave the room. It took repeated requests from Dr. Thomas before the attending nurses began to come back to themselves and their duties, to take the disfigured, dark purple child from the doctor's hands and perform the routine task of cutting the umbilical cord.

By all other accounts, this was a normal birth for the mother. Perhaps this was a dream, nothing more than fears left to burgeon into fantasy? But no, not this time. A quick nod of acknowledgment from Don and the decision was made to delay showing the mother her child.

"I want to see my baby," Norma cried. Something was horribly wrong. She knew it. Even through the discomfort of having just given birth, she was aware of the glimpses darting between the figures that stood round her bed. But nobody was prepared to answer her pleas.

"Mrs. Carter, we have to take your son immediately…for his safety," explained the nurse, but her eyes refused to meet Norma's own.

* * *

It would only be much later in life that there would be some understanding of the child's condition. In 1959, there was only a medical "assessment," a "description," if you will, to point out the child's defects, which were extreme in nature by any standards. Please understand that these kinds of cases are rare at best, so their conditions are rarely understood. In those days, there were few corrections to pursue. Therefore, it would be left to the child, much, much later, to attempt to understand the reason, the effects, and the consequences of the abnormal body with which he had been saddled. Only much, much later would there be knowledge to challenge a persisting mental "condition" as well. For now, however, the deformed, grotesque figure was described as follows, according to Dr. Thomas, attending physician:

What appears to be a fetal congenital disfigurement of all external limbs and members associated. Includes: left leg inward turned and clubfooted with missing extension of all toes. The larger toe considered fused and webbed onto the second toe with extra flaps of tissue and deficient of all nails.

Knee and ankle formation is lacking extension and the tendon appears to be absent. Foot considered the stronger of the two; however, faces reconstruction in some manner. Thigh has firm muscle and appears correctly developed through to hip.

Right leg, all associated members have extensive damage and distortion. The foot is of a form similar to that of a large thumb or extended limb and has no other toe or limb digits visible. The webbing is extreme and covers well into the calf region, which appears to be absent all muscle and tendon arrangement.

The foot turned inward and has a degree greater than 90 inside value. The knee joint is mobile yet articulate and rotated. Femur bone be the only bone construct and would not be able to sustain as

a weight-bearing limb in this condition.

Ankle mobility amalgamated and the grotesque nature of this

limb suggests amputation. Thigh muscular arrangement is small in

comparison to left leg; includes mass of webbing and tissue buildup

behind knee joint, suggesting growth of extremities below are absent

nerve and normal vascular progress. More to be

discussed/consultation required.

Hip proportional to pelvis and lower back suggest contorted at

best; will need surgical alignment. Fetus shows normal and

functional genitalia. Torso appears to have distorted outline; organs

shifted in alignment with emphasis on heart-lung cavities. Distended

heart; chest wall suggests possible heart-lung deformities and want

further attention. All vital signs stable.

Left arm appears to be functional from shoulder down to wrist

with range of motion normal. Left hand particularly webbed and deformed with thumb and index rather normal. All remaining digits

appear distorted, deformed, or absent. Middle and second digits are

missing from second knuckle and fused together both in skin and

bone composition. Last finger is webbed and all have narrow

movement. Growth of nail development is absent on middle digit,

and distorted third and fourth with no sign of motion range on

either. More consultation needed. Right appendage is severe and

reflects entire right side of body as malformed. Arm webbed from

approx. shoulder to wrist with what appears to be no muscular

development from elbow up. Indication of functional distortion,

further consultation needed. Right hand entirely covered in

excessive skin and tissue. Right thumb and index fingers fused and

webbed. Thumb appears to be absent joint one. Index is absent from

second knuckle beyond. Middle and second be normal and stable in

development. Small latter digit inhibited by what appears to be a

band of constrained skin. Blood and restricted movement; wants

further consultation. Range of motion and use of this arm is constrained at best and considered for amputation. Fusion of joint and capacity to use full extension is limited and underdeveloped.

Head and neck normal and have full range of motion with little conflict. Facial and cranium bones with eye, nose, and mouth conform to expected normal appearance. Ear development is normal on both sides with minor lack of skin and curvature on top of left, not expected to affect future external or internal use. All early cavity search checks unambiguous with no visible deformation. Facial appearance considered excellent.

All other physical abnormalities as seen or not, is to be further discussed and reviewed subject to future discoveries.

First assessment assumes all skeletal and muscular development will need extensive corrective measures to follow. Fetus suffers from extreme congenital confinement defects limited to no further role without far-reaching tries at prosthesis or reconstruction.

At preliminary stage, I would consider this fetus exceedingly disfigured, not able to walk or work without support or custodial care for some time, if at all.

It is this observer's opinion based on medical knowledge only: fetus is and should be considered for possible exclusion. As previously understood, child has not been presented to Mother. In addition, there is no known treatment or course of correction! Immediate rectification with intensive equipped procedures will be required of the fetus that is outside the scope of this facility's knowledge and ability. Transfer of accounts and patient suggested. Consultation required.

Dictated by Dr. Thomas, September 1, 1959 – 11:35 pm

It would be long into the next day before all involved were made aware of the conditions as explained by Dr. Thomas. The waiting room went silent. What was there to say? They had all known the possibilities that this pregnancy could bring, but now their fears had been realized. It was not until later that first day that Dr. Thomas had begun to assemble a group of his peers to consult with him on this perplexing case, but he had talked with Norma Jean and Donny and provided his medical observations. The only thing that was clear was that this was completely new territory for the lot of them.

The hours that followed passed in slow motion, each member of the family treading ever so cautiously so as not to give vent to the anger, frustration, and sadness building inside. The urge to lash out was strong, however, and it took all their effort to meet the task head-on while listening to so many strangers discuss what had transpired. Faith and pride were being tested to a point of fracture. This family had never claimed freedom from strife and surpassing the point of pain had always been a fact of life. But this time, in their shame and guilt, life was dealing them a blow that would take every ounce of support they could offer one another. The question in their heads went around and around: What had they done to deserve this? This was a question which would haunt them for the rest of their lives.

Chapter 8

SEVENTY-TWO HOURS OF LIFE

On the morning of day three, the tears had all since dried up. Together medical professionals, parents, and grandparents accompanied the new family to listen to Dr. Thomas. Explaining his recommendations to the group, Dr. Thomas knew his words revealed the angst he felt. Numb from exhaustion, he knew decisions had to be made quickly, and that Don's presence in the room meant he would have the final say.

"Good morning, everyone. What I am going to tell you, after having consulted with the other doctors, will be difficult to hear. I have to warn you that the information we have is critical. First, the child is doing well and is resting as well as can be expected. I'm sure by now you have had the chance to see him and know that he is an exceptional and beautiful baby boy."

"He gets that from me!" said the proud father, and everyone laughed nervously, trying to dispel the aura of thick grief in the room. Then they waited for the rest of the news.

Not one to refuse solid advice from those whom he trusted, Don knew he needed to listen, needed to hear whatever the doctor had to say, and then be quick to assure Norma that all had been taken care of. The next step was to find a solution.

Dr. Thomas continued. "Well, I'm glad to hear you have a smile in your heart for this child. I think we can do much good for him. Perhaps, and I say that with caution, perhaps if we do, we will be able to give him a somewhat normal and productive life. Nevertheless, it's going to take a lot of work and we need to start immediately. With that said, Norma, Don, we recommend that to start we place your son inside a cast, a full-body cast. The constraint of the cast will aggressively allow his frail bones to move into a position that will later make the task of rebuilding easier. Currently, we need time to collect information and research our choices. Although we have all agreed," the doctor said, turning to include the men behind him, "our best chance is to use restrictive traction, such as one would use for a broken bone."

Flossie was quick to voice her question. "Are you saying you're going to break the little angel's bones and then cast them?"

One of the other white-smocked men answered, "No, not right now, anyway. Our hope is that the form of the cast will allow his defective bones to move into position, the way a broken arm or leg can do. Frankly, it's the only thing we can do until we are sure he is stable enough to perform reconstruction."

Dr. Thomas continued with a nod. "We know it may seem hard to understand, but this child has presented us with a situation unlike anything any of us have ever seen at this hospital. There was one other similar case, which was quickly sent to Riley's and then St. Vincent's in Indianapolis. Our research is leading us to recommend you there as well. However, we feel that time is of the essence. I expect to have more information later today and at that point I will want to speak with you and your family further. For now, though, do I have your approval to continue? I can tell you that should we not continue, the child's bones will continue to strengthen into their current position. It is the only choice we have, Norma."

All eyes turned to Norma and Don, who had grasped Norma's hand in his. Norma gave a quick nod of agreement. The thought of her son engulfed in a prison of plaster before ever knowing the feel of freedom and the idea of never seeing the joy of her son's capacities was crushing her to the point of collapse. Knowing the people around her were stronger than she at that moment, she simply waved to signal she wanted to be alone. The crowd began to exit, their expressions grave but optimistic about the outcome of this first effort. They wondered what would be next, but again silently agreed to hold their tongues.

* * *

An hour later, in a room filled with instruments and the cold steel table of medical devices, a small figure lay immersed in a bath of water. Cotton, plaster, and tools more comfortably seen in a workshop surrounded the child, now under bright lights. Never had any of the doctors been so challenged, and each one who touched this boy's life would do so with heartfelt pain. The wrap of material slowly entrapped the small body with each lap around the skin. The performers could not help it; they wanted to look away but could not. As if spoken aloud, the single thought rang out over and over: God, what have you done? The doctors dared not look at each other for fear that a flaw would appear in their demeanor. With each layer, wrapping, wrapping, entrapping, the infant beseeched them for an answer, an explanation. But there was none to give.

How would this child understand? The tears shed that morning were not the child's, but of those in attendance. When the last bit of wrapping had been applied and the last fold conformed to the shape determined best, the three-day-old body was successfully enveloped in a white prison of hell. With photos and recorders in place, each step of the event was noted for review, and the hardened mass of plaster lay still upon the platform. Soon it was wheeled into a single room to remain separate from all others.

* * *

The years of segregation and discrimination had begun. Nobody wished

for it, certainly, and perhaps no one understood how it happened. But,

when presented with the facts, the question was surely how—or better,

if—there was even the slightest chance that the outcome for such a child,

with any amount of corrective measures, could be altered. Surely if there

ever was a time for a redo, this would be it. But who are we to question

the methods of God? Who are we to ask if such an abomination is truly a

child of God? But how could He allow such a mistake to happen? After

all, what could possibly be in store for such a child? Could this instead be

called a phenomenon?

Were these the questions of those involved—or would they become the

questions of the child? Perhaps some would say that there is a better world

beyond; I would have to say, at what cost? And who defines the

punishment? For now, barely the size of a telephone, the child lay

helpless, buried alive inside a stark white plaster in a cold dark room with

no way out.

85

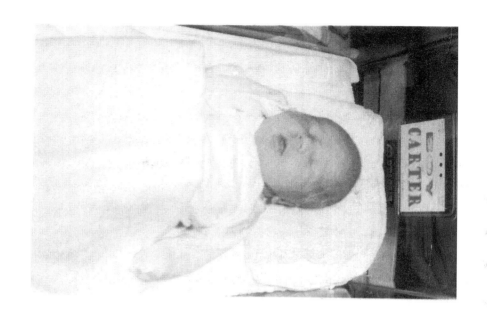

Chapter 9

COLLECTION OF TIME

On day four, the tasks seemed endless. No singular solution presented itself, even with an entire family and staff of medical personnel at the feet of the small cause. By now, Norma had been released to go home if she wished. With her only child captured and held, however, there was but one place to be. Her pain remained invisible to most. She had been taught well by the women before her how a matriarch was to behave and by then it had become instinct. No one would see the tears she cried inside.

Don did what he knew how to do, and he went about it with single-minded purpose. He would work, work to ensure his family would be as strong and financially secure as possible. This was not a man to succumb to resistance, no matter its origin.

Dr. Thomas spoke to the young couple daily. "I want to assure you that we are all doing the best we can, Norma, Don. I have placed a call to have your son expedited to a specialist who deals with these types of…difficulties. His name is Dr. Karl Martz. He is known as the one of the best orthopedic surgeons in the country." Dr. Thomas spoke with a confidence to disguise the heavy layer of fear he held.

"Please be honest with us, Doctor. What should we do? Do we need to go see this doctor or will he come here?" Norma asked.

"I cannot say for sure, Norma, but according to his receptionist we do know that he is able and interested in meeting with you. I should know something later today."

"Can I hold my son today?" Norma wanted to know. "Can't I pick him up and touch him?"

Dr. Thomas paused. It was with sincere regret that he then said, "No, Norma, I'm sorry. But he will be out of these casts in less than a week and we should have a clear idea about what we need to do then. I know this is painful and hard to endure, but I can only ask you to have faith and believe we are doing our best."

Later that day what was to become the familiar sight of a lonely soldier of a woman standing in front of a glass window could be seen. Perhaps her thoughts were of guilt and remorse for not barring this child's entrance to the world. Perhaps she thought she was being punished for her family's choices. The questions, without answers, paved a long road, one she would travel every day of the rest of her life.

* * *

Except for the sound of the women's heels tapping the tiles, the hallways of the hospital were long and quiet. The two figures, elegantly dressed and proper, approached Norma's side. By now, Hildreth and Flossie had become the tapestry of support for their little girl and her son. They had silently agreed to become a force of one, to assist wherever needed, in these most difficult of circumstances.

"How do you feel today, Norma Jean?" Hildreth asked. "Your doctor said he released you. Are you planning on going home later?"

When Norma didn't answer, Flossie tried again. "He's an angel, you know, dear. Look at those blue eyes. Those are his father's in him, you know." Flossie said this with pride.

The women clucked nervously, watching the baby who lay in tranquil stillness, disturbed only by the occasional nurse who came to check on him and perform routine tasks. The minutes turned to hours; the conversation lagged until it finally ended altogether. The coffee was refreshed time and time again, as Norma continued to repel the attempted hug or the touch of a hand, knowing she was not able to grant her son the same. It was not until late that night when Don came to sit with her that she released her hold on the day to go home and rest.

This would be the first of many nights alone for Norma Jean. Her world was a world of the normal and the proper; it was not supposed to be like this. Her son was supposed to be strong, to have all the gifts this world had to offer. Damn you, God, damn you… Those were the words that rang in Norma Jean's head. In a society that frowned on all things different, all things outside the status quo, the mountain ahead seemed unbearably hard to climb. God had abandoned her and left her this deformed responsibility.

In the weeks that followed, the child's prognosis became a little more optimistic. The doctors had reached a joint agreement regarding their program for the next six months and the first of many operations to come.

By the age of one year, the small body had undergone four reconstruction and/or removal procedures. The webbing from the right arm and hand had been trimmed to reveal a more functional set of digits. Amputation to remove the entire lower half of the right leg had been considered on and off, but never implemented. In addition, there was serious consideration given to the idea of installing a mechanical device that could serve as a finger or a thumb. Dr. Martz was aggressive, but Norma was persistent and these innovations went undone. The general conclusion was that this child had shown enough strength, even in his silence, to overcome the hurdles ahead.

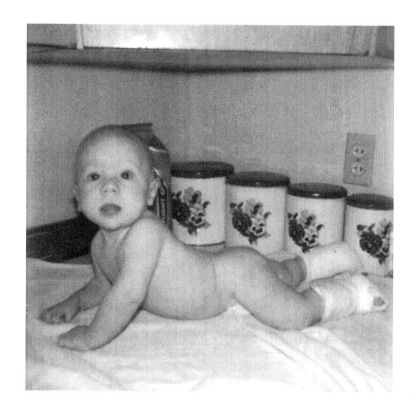

By now, Don had secured his position in the family business in Indianapolis and moved his wife and child into a small house not far from Norma's parents, who had also relocated. Don's uncle had made it clear that the family was there for him and would help in whatever way they could. For Donny, however, memories of the little house down the alley were never far away.

"Donnie, we love you and this is where we want you to be," his Uncle Arnold told him with firm compassion. "Nevertheless, your dad's drinking…jail…that's all in the past. We have a good life here and we wish the same for you, too. You have a big job ahead of you with a crippled child."

"I understand," said Don, and he did. He knew that this was the just the beginning.

It was not long after moving to Indianapolis that Don became less present in the daily affairs of the home and more involved with his work. Norma took on the chores of running the house and the care of her much-restricted child. The years passed. It was November 22, 1963. The body of a child, wrapped in a familiar sight of casting and plaster, was lying on the floor. In the background, the sounds of daily housekeeping tasks filled the home with an atmosphere of a simple life. Popeye's craggy voice could be heard, and the amused, canned laughter that accompanied it.

* * *

I was drawing pictures of friends and coloring in my book of dreams. I had recently returned home from the first of what was to be three more surgeries. My right foot had been completely rebuilt, bones broken or removed, tendons extended, stretched, and manipulated to conform to a position that might possibly support weight in the future. The foot had taken on a look of a grotesque alien. Having been made painfully aware of how my appearance affected others, my mother was always quick to disguise my extremities when others were around. She did not have to worry about that right now, though. All was right with her world while she was safe within the confines of her home. It was a crisp fall day on a quiet street in America.

I remember lying on the floor and crawling to the couch. The mood had shifted. I watched as my mother cry uncontrollably. I felt, perhaps for the first time consciously, that I was the cause of her pain. It seemed the world had once again passed judgment against her for something I had done, for what I was. After all, I was the problem. I am the one who did not have fingers, toes, and legs like yours! It would not be for many years that I would appreciate that the events shown that day on television were responsible for her state, not me. It seemed like my mother cried for hours.

As I rolled or waddled from position to position, day after day, I began to take comfort in my simple imaginary friends who either sat next to me or appeared in a color or as a line on a page. How I wish I might have known what my mother's pain was about that day. I thought it was about me. I always thought it was about me…

These were my first memories. I consider this period of my life critical for that reason. Events like these shaped me, made me who I am today. My world ran in parallel to everyone else's; my life was almost predictable in a way that others' were not. As unlikely as it may sound to some, even at the age of four I understood that each moment had a value.

Many years later as an adult, I learned that there were a number of well-dressed women who came to my hospital rooms periodically to offer me a stuffed animal or toy. One of these women was named Ruth. There were many others. To this day I am inspired to buy stuffed animals for the children around me. I spent every summer bound and restricted in casts for the next five years. The challenge of watching the world play from the confines of a blanket, from behind a window, would isolate my mind and heart.

By the time I reached the age of nine, I had had over fifteen reconstructive surgeries and extensions. They used feline tendons to extend my calf and ankles. I had another extension in my right arm to enable my arm to straighten. That surgery failed after three attempts.

My mother made many changes in her life to accommodate the
circumstances, and playing the Cub Scout den-mother was only one of her
many efforts to include her otherwise excluded son. I can remember on
many occasions begging her not take me or to quit the Cub Scouts
altogether. Even though I earned a couple of badges and ribbons, I never
accepted the quiet whispers and stares that came with public or social
situations. But because my attendance seemed to bring honor to my Dad, I

carried on. By this time in my life, the way people talked, asked, and stared was nothing new. Though I had come to expect it, their words and questions felt like an invasion each time, but I did not show the hurt. Somewhere, somehow, I had developed or a high tolerance for pain. I also learned that tolerance can be confused with callousness to justify ignorance.

Somewhere amid our struggles to remake my body, my father found the time to be successful in his acquisition of money and fame in his trade. On or around my ninth birthday I was entered in a Pinewood Derby contest. I was enrolled in school during the fall and winter months; during the summer I had all my operations.

I remember two events that included my Dad. One of them I only remembered after being shown a picture in which he was lying on the floor with me, playing with a miniature army. The second was the Pinewood Derby contest. There was to be no second-place finish. In the weeks prior, my dad took me to his engineering and tool shop where his world existed in exact thousandths' of fractions, in precise instruments and foreign sounds. For me it was always a feeling of being less than, exaggerated by the comparison of my failed body to the precision instruments and creations built there. Nonetheless, I was excited just to be at his side. I did not care about the race. In fact, I did not even understand what we were doing because my dad had entered the race for me. I recall sitting on a stool, watching, amazed that this man was my dad. Strong, tall, and proud, he was someone I did not know except in dreams or at the occasional dinner. I think I was the one whose pride should have been recognized that night.

"Do you think we could win second or third maybe, Dad?" I asked him, knowing I did not deserve first.

"Son, there is no such thing as second, there is only first. Don't forget that!"

I never did forget my father's words, even though I have tried many times since to understand the consequences of that statement.

Those poor kids stood watching my father and me, wrapped again and held in place by shiny metal that weighed more than my entire body. The colorful homemade boxy black-wheeled toy moved ever so sluggishly down the narrow track, the lead-weighted, precision ground-racing wheel aero-tool for which I was responsible already steadied for the next challenger. I felt sorry for the other kids, but I dared not show that concern to my dad. It was his moment of glory for his crippled son. Nobody challenged or denied the award, but we never entered again and from that day forward the trophy sat for all to see.

Perhaps the experience of seeing my father's workplace enlightened me as to what was happening to my body in some way. I have always slept with a pair of metal shoes connected to either the bed itself or to a heavy strap of steel. My nights were filled with tears and cries of tortured pain. My arms were often secured as well to prevent movement or enable motion. As a child, I experienced the confines of my own personal insane asylum. Perhaps most children escape, enjoy the play-land of a room filled with toys in their dreams. I never dreamed between the walls of my concealment. A refuge or haven it was not.

One of the most memorable aspects was the smell. I can to this day describe the smell of flesh or scar tissue. It is as unique a smell I have ever encountered, one which has offered a peculiar sense of identity, or perhaps an eccentric personal awareness.

I do recall the excitement when the family moved into a new house. The anticipation was huge. Since it was being constructed in winter, we were allowed to visit and roam about while the walls were uncovered. Our relationship with my father's extended family had been growing as well through the years and I loved them all.

Christmas was a discovery of new scents and colorful packages tucked under the silver tree. Whether from need or based purely on family connection, I always had a wonderful time visiting Uncle Arwood and Aunt Mary, with their children's playful acceptance of us—of me. Later, as we only reunited at funerals, I would miss this connection.

It was not long before I started to assert my own identity and develop a

bit of a rebellious attitude. Perhaps I was resistant to the religious training

of a God who had carelessly created me, or perhaps I began to feel

privileged, but my father's strict lifestyle did not include a smart-mouthed

kid. My mother had since introduced me, despite objection by my father,

to the methodical belief that God was a forgiving and loving presence.

This did not ring true for me. It also seemed to me that my father's original attempts at being a part of my life were methodically being replaced with guidelines too strict to follow. I never did understand how our lives appeared one way outside the door and another on the inside.

Once the house was complete, we moved in. We lived in one of the nicest areas of town and established ourselves as part of the upper crust. Everything was first-class, a home in the suburbs and a car to match. Our lives appeared safe and normal. By now my mother was enjoying a successful real estate position that offered her many avenues of freedom from the difficulties she faced at home. In the spring of 1969, our life was complete; with all this effort surely our suffering was over. At least my parents', anyway.

A number of experiences shaped my opinion of how others viewed me while we lived on this street. On one of those occasions, I was on my way home from school. My arm was in a cast and I was in leg braces, as always, something which did not keep me from class most of the time. The braces were loud and noisy, always interfering with others' space and inhibiting silence. A couple of the boys followed me home, teasing me, calling me names. They were a lot bigger than I was.

"Hey, Freak, Shrimp, Stubby!" they yelled, knocking my books out from under my other, uncasted arm.

I said the only thing I knew. "Please, leave me alone. I didn't do anything to you."

Obviously my mother had been watching from afar—as perhaps she always had? This time I heard, "Hit 'em, Kris, hit 'em back!"

I blinked in astonishment. I had never failed to follow her advice, but this had come from left field. Confused, but used to doing what I was told, I swung to hit them. Losing my balance, I fell to the ground. I tried repeatedly to grab at something, anything to regain balance and pick myself up, but each time I was hit again or simply knocked over like a bobble toy. I wept and sobbed with each effort until my mother finally came to scatter the boys.

I never stopped wondering whether the fear and pain they inflicted that day had affected those boys. Were they guilt-ridden, knowing what they had done? Or had it been easy to forget? My pain, on the other hand, which never went away, was nothing more than another ache to live with.

Across the street lived a family of boys who were my age. I recall the many times during the summer I stood at the edge of the fence to watch them swim in the in-ground pool in their backyard. It smelled from afar of the clean scents of life and energy. I had never enjoyed the water except at the hospital pool when they took me for therapy. I had all the normal young boy attitudes and beliefs, or so I thought. Why couldn't I swim with the others? Somehow, my mother caught wind of my desire and managed to arrange for me to do just that. Unfortunately, the looks on the kids' faces as they stared at my deformities and spoke in quiet whispers was another reminder that in fact I was all too different. I am equally sure that it was an overwhelming experience for my mother. I wish I had understood then. I guess I was just the spoiled rich crippled kid in the neighborhood. Oh, how I grew to hate that word, *crippled.*

My dad bought us a little motorcycle, a Honda 50. Mind you, I was at best three-foot tall with one arm that I could not use. We had a picnic table in the back of our yard that abutted against the field of a church. I learned to stand on the table, lean the motorbike against the wood and climb aboard. I learned how to fall! But soon I had figured out how to coast ever so softly up to the table and lean over enough to get on and off all by myself. Our life in this new home was young, but good. Strict, too. There were no shoes in the dining room and every Sunday we clipped the grass from the edge of our drive. Perhaps we had found happiness.

I only wished that happiness was within me. I know that most of you who read this will struggle with, perhaps even reject, the idea that I have lived my entire life feeling as if an existence as Frankenstein was my only fate in life. But since I can recall, I have had the overwhelming desire that when I met someone new, he will look me in the eye and not be compelled or distracted to look at my body, my hands, or the metal equipment supporting them.

As a child, my family made it very clear that I should not pay attention to this reaction, and that I should consider myself special. I understand that approach; it is the one I would use, too, if I found myself in their shoes.

107

Nevertheless, today, isolated and alone in a world where normalcy is measured in terms of visual perfection, an abnormal figure, a hand that scares the person shaking it, only means a sense of disconnection for its bearer. Throughout my childhood, I not only knew I was different, but every day I knew that I was second- or third-class—at best.

As a result, I created a false identity, one that I hoped would make me appear larger, bigger in attitude, more intimidating. I tried often, but continued to fall decidedly short of my goal. It would not be until much later and after much failure that I would find a solution to the emotional scars left by my trying to fit in. If only I might have heeded the words of my wise mother when she said, "This too shall pass," words she used to remind me of our blessings on every occasion—whether they applied or not.

Family reunions took place at our house and were filled with food and love. J. P. was eagerly working on completing his first phase of the cabin at Trail's End in hopes of having the next reunion there. Everyone had come to accept the past, though there was an ever-present undercurrent of gentle concern for future generations to come. In previous years, we gathered in the car to go visit Grandma Flossie and the small dairy, but big ice-cream store, next door. Flossie was always quick to greet us when we arrived. I can still see the signs along the way, the last one's appearance indicating we had made it safely. The backyard was filled with grapevines and the smell of blossoms ready to unfold for the jellies or jams to come. Once, when visiting, a man whom I later came to know as Uncle Bill was there. Seems we all have an Uncle Bill. It struck me as odd when I learned he was Grandma's son. Uncle Bill was accompanied by a man who spoke little and carried a black case; not a friendly man. I later learned that Uncle Bill often visited a place called Havana. He is said to have died in the Philippines, and the stories say he was a CIA agent, that he knew a little something about that day Mom cried years ago.

We used to visit Martha Rose and my cousins as well. I remember my Uncle Herb, too, a huge, strong man who built houses. I later fell from my cousins' grace, but at that time they were always willing to tolerate the crippled kid. I didn't know then the impact of our relationships and how they had made adjustments to accommodate me. I am grateful to them for their kindness, and the kindness of their mother, my Aunt Diane, truly one of the most gracious women I have ever met. Other than family, I never really had any friends. I think it was because nobody knew how to relate to someone so different in a world full of same. In this world, should they have had to? It took far too much effort to be involved with a kid with braces.

Either way, I found myself astonished when I encountered one of the people I'd known back then and he actually remembered me as a child. I believe there was both shock and compassion in his eyes. Perhaps he was one of the kids who came and sat on the blanket with me under the tree on long warm afternoons. Perhaps these children had been told to "go sit with the poor little boy," but either way it was appreciated. To be truthful, though, I only felt as if I belonged when I was with other kids who were sick or deformed like me.

When we went to Dr. Martz's office other children were often there, but I do not remember ever seeing another with as many metal braces or casts. I always enjoyed meeting and talking with them, though, because in those moments I did not feel alone, even for a moment. I believe it is easier to understand the temporary isolation that comes from an illness or an emotional setback, but isolation that is unremitting takes on an identity of its own, a substance, if you will. I never learned how to talk fluidly or socialize normally with others, the ones I saw as having all the things in life freely offered to them, all the things I had been denied. Sure, I was intelligent and understood language; in fact, I would excel to the point of having no avenue of expression for the things I felt. It was the mid-sixties then, and to be an American meant getting a job in a factory and working hard for thirty years until it was time to retire. This was the recipe for happiness. I understood that it may be true for all the others, but not for me.

Half of my body not only did not work, but was numb and determined to be useless without support. How could I ever be a part of something with which I had no connection? Denied even the basics of normalcy, I didn't belong; I was a misfit.

You might say I felt sorry for myself. Or perhaps that I needed help. You might pass judgment and decide that I deserved whatever came to me. All I can tell you is that in my world there have been so few like me that help and understanding is at best a guess. How could anyone understand? Escape from reality was a daily chore, an exercise in control. I lay lifeless and separate from the people touching me, while the hard leather-bound shoes with bolts and screws extending from their soles and sides were forced onto my legs. I prayed for the exercise to conclude, never wanting it to begin again. I listened to the crash and clink of steel bars against my skin, bitterly aware that they represented my only hope for walking. It became all too apparent that I would have to completely accept the fact that my body and my life would never function on its own, that I would always need the assistance of someone or something else.

That attitude and the need to find release led me into the next era of my life. I had begun to expand on my personal method of escape, which utilized pencil, paper, and paint as a mode of expression. Grasping a writing device was difficult, and manipulating the curve or angle of even a simple letter presented pain and frustrations most will never know. I was nine with the body of a fifty-year-old, or so it felt.

Norma, with the humor of recognition and an overprotective nature, was always quick with praise. In truth, she was my best friend, my only real companion for many years. I didn't have to explain anything; there were no questions to answer, no justification to provide. When asked, "What happened to you?" I came to realize that the best answer was "it." "That's the way *it* was at birth, that's the way God wanted *it* to be."

The word "it" became a mandated personal reference.

Chapter 10

TIME TO CHANGE

Not knowing the crime committed, I was surprised one typical summer day when our world changed again. That morning was filled with tension and tears as my mother and Grandma Hildreth packed boxes that soon lined the hall. I found myself in the way so I retreated to my room. Recently, the last triple ortho-reconstruction of my right foot had been completed. This time the surgery was extensive and I bled for many days. I was under anesthesia for many hours and had bled through at least three casts. I heard many years later that I had had to be resuscitated during the process. Not having the strength or muscle to carry such a heavy plaster block around, I was now using a crutch with bracing that bolted onto my legs and hips to allow me some moderate form of independent movement. When the large truck appeared, it was clear that I was to follow Norma out the front door.

I wish I could tell you the truth of that period of my life, but I cannot. Stories surfaced that suggested my father had an affair. Right or wrong, personal escape, or egotistical play? I don't know. It is my personal belief that we are responsible for our lives, for where we find ourselves in those lives. At some point, at some time, we consciously or subconsciously make choices that result in our current position. Ironic perhaps from coming from someone who had no choice in the beginning stages of his life.

I knew that I would never live with my dad again in the comfort he provided. Later that night, in a mobile home cluttered with assorted open containers, my mother and her mother sat talking long into the night at a metal table with chairs as shiny as my legs. We spent the next few weeks there. Dad came by occasionally to visit, but never stayed.

I recall we had a plan if anyone tried to break in. Mom had a baseball bat at the ready. I was supposed to flip on the lights. Unbelievably, such a night actually occurred. Startled awake and stricken with fear at the sounds of a screen door crashing, I was unable to move from my bed. I later learned that my father had showed up drunk at the door in hopes of talking to Mom. That was the last time. Don was about to exit Norma's life forever.

* * *

On a hot day humid from the Indiana sun, I came out from my bedroom to see a man sitting inside my mother's kitchen. I had never seen such a person before. I was shy with concern for my mother's safety.

"Don't be frightened, Kris, I want you to meet a friend of mine. His name is Johnny."

Before me stood a man in a uniform that announced his presence with loud bold colors across his broad chest. Trim and neat, with a voice deep and firm, he said, "Pleasure to meet you, son."

I stood, quietly repulsed by the words this man used, and then escaped into the mental seclusion I had perfected. I would not appear again for many years to come. I politely excused myself and retreated to my room, not ready to believe that another man had entered our lives. I understood Norma's need to the degree a child could, but I did not understand her request of me. Was I to accept without reservation or compromise all that had been taught to me? Would I now not only be a freak of nature, but unwillingly transformed into another man's son? I did not understand my role. Here stood a United States Marine Corps Drill Instructor who intimidated me to my core. I feared even looking at this man and had no idea how to talk to him or what to say.

The next couple of weeks went by quickly. Johnny's thirty-day leave was ending and Mom took me aside to announce she was going to marry this man. I had been spending a lot of time at my grandmother's house in Muncie since Johnny had appeared, and it seemed that our lives were falling back to where they had begun.

What once before seemed like a world of endless—if unlikely—possibilities now became small and secluded. Introduced to new terms, such as "step-cousin," I was distrustful and refused to accept this new turn of events. Gathering to go to the county fair, we walked down the same dirty Midway alleys through which so many had strolled before. I resented the excitement.

I felt as though I were on display. The gawking, the laughing, the stares, and whispers grew louder with every pass of a stranger. Between leaving all that I knew—a comfortable home with two parents—and my physical isolation, I had reached the end of my tether. I rebelled with a violence and anger that had been suppressed for years.

All my life I had been the quiet, protected, humble, "strong" young boy who endured strife and misery with little complaint. Dealing with poverty now as well, new struggles beyond my world as it had existed began to surface. Someday, I knew I would exorcise the pain I felt, a pain no man or woman should have to experience. I was accused of being spoiled and isolated from reality; my accusers were correct. I found myself not wanting to speak and even made manipulative efforts to undermine and confuse my mother's new relationship.

It took many years for me to come to understand Johnny and Norma's lifelong connection and how it had evolved. At the time of their wedding ceremony, however, the one I witnessed from the sidelines when the two of them were joined as one, I knew nothing but my own misery. Even though they explained to me in words about divorce, I had no conception of what that really meant, or the capacity to draw certain conclusions. At age nine, within the confines of the small social bubble of a world I had managed to explore, there was no divorce, only the sudden appearance of an entirely new group of adults and children to whom I had no previous connection.

We moved again, this time to government family housing on a military base. To me, it was yet another penalty I deserved. I knew it was my fault. I had caused the break up of my family. I felt my mother would be much happier without me in her life. In reality, Norma's pain was severe as well, as she grasped for security and fought her own demons. I celebrated my

120

tenth birthday with my new family in the three-room house. It was a poor neighborhood in town, just on the other side of those same tracks other generations had feared to cross on their way to the fair...

On that day, we traveled as a collection of strangers to the dusty Midway. I found myself torn between feeling like an example of lost fame and a disfigured inclusion into a life not understood. As we walked the channels where previous feet had left footprints in the dirt, my view was limited to the path in front of me to prevent a stumble or fall. I had never experienced this kind of despair. Never had I thought the kind of words that now flooded my head in constant accompaniment to my lurching step. It was as if my deformed body had been captured by a distorted soul over the last months. No safe harbor or vessel to declare home, I had always known what it felt like not to belong. Now I longed for an escape to fill the void left by this distraction from what had become my normal, invisible separation from human contact. God, give me relief from the future!

Chapter 11

CALIFORNIA

The plane landed in a fury of noise, knocked about like a toy. I was excited and anxious. Our flight from safety into the dangers of the entire world opened in a flash as we exited the cabin door. I had never experienced anything like it before. The air was thick enough to touch, but there was nothing I could see, no puff of breath of the kind I was used to seeing. The warm air coated my skin with a damp sensation. Norma Jean seemed as excited as I was. We were standing at the entrance of a large room when her husband Johnny, as I called him, entered. My efforts at walking and running in joy were interrupted when he spoke, "Hello, Kris, what did you think of the plane ride?"

My reaction was calculatingly cold and I replied only with a disrespectful, "Fine." I would soon learn that disrespect would not be an avenue of the lesser evils in this new collection of strangers.

Not long after we arrived in California, I began to look for ways to entertain myself. By now the rage and frustration within me was intense and ever-present, but I had very little understanding about why I was feeling this way. My mother had had all my supplies sent out ahead so I had everything I needed. I soon found another kid who was willing to set aside judgment in pursuit of mutual interest and benefit and it was not long before we were stealing fishing lures from the local store, and selling them to the anglers down at the fishing pier in San Diego. The rush of adrenalin that came with each theft filled that angry empty space temporarily. I also had my first exposure to someone who would become a longtime friend, someone who seemed not to care what I looked like or what I could or could not do. This "friend" didn't talk to me, but did much of the hard work for me. At the age of ten I smoked my first joint. I am not sure how to explain the experience other than to say that marijuana made me feel equal. All of a sudden I was not the kid with the freak shoes in the braces and the missing fingers. I wasn't any of that any more! All of a sudden, I was as good as everyone else.

Looking back, I see that my mother and her new husband had an extreme challenge ahead of them, one which I had no business trying to sabotage. Nevertheless, I was lost, believing I had no one on whom to depend, other than my mother—and she was caught up in her new marriage. My dad was gone, my Grandma, everyone who understood, all the family members who would come to the rescue if there was ever a problem. Suddenly they were two thousand miles away; how could they help us now? We were on our own.

The doctors had performed seventeen or eighteen surgeries by now and there was really nothing left to be done; my body was as good as it was going to get. Like a broken dish never to completely useful again, I felt abandoned. I still wore braces of heavy metal with leather shoes and a corrective brace I slept with every single night. I had steel-toed shoes before they were in fashion.

It was just before we left to come to California that I had one of my last casts removed. I can tell you that throughout my entire life I never forgot the horrendous sound of that electric saw cutting the casts off my legs and arms. The fear that seared through me every time I heard that saw start up with its deafening buzz sent me into uncontrollable sobs. Oddly enough, that experience was in direct contrast with the doctors who used to touch my body, with their soft warm compassionate hands. I almost felt privileged in those moments.

Over the next few months, my mother introduced me to some people about whom I had only heard stories, like her brother Charles who lived in a place called Palm Springs. Charles' place had the feel of a far-away land, a kind of sanctuary that offered safety to those who understood. The drive was always long and hot, with little or no signs of life that I could recognize. The desert is a vast place for a small child, but by now I had developed a tougher shell and was more agile handling myself. The limits of my physical constraints, not having any sensation from the knees down, become less important relative to our activities. It was not long before we started to take trips to Los Angles to visit a woman named Martha and a man called Tom. It seemed that another family we knew had emerged from the sand.

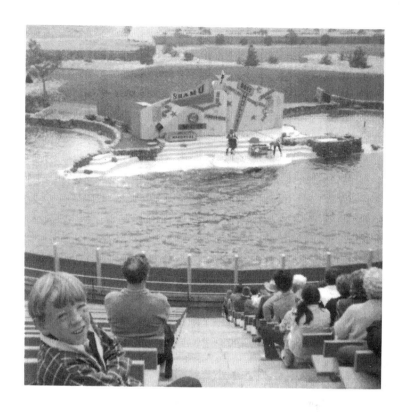

My deceits and wrongdoings were as yet still undiscovered by my
mother. I found endless opportunities at amusement parks, places called
Knott's Berry Farm, Sea World, and Disney Land. These were places
where I could go and feel comfortable and I flitted between the crowds of
strangers, dissolving into the shadow-masses. Every turn was filled with
fantasy and illusion. It was a world without flaws—a far cry from the local
fair back in Indiana.

Even though Norma was often distracted (by what I later learned were her own fears), she was constantly attending to my needs as well as a new bride could. In these times of distraction, I was aware that my behavior and attitude became intolerable, and the short-haired, tanned man we now lived with was quick to point that out. To this day, I am nothing short of amazed at how loving, compassionate, and caring these two adults were, though I could not see evidence of this at the time.

We lived in a place called Chula Vista and I attended a school in National City. The heavy Spanish influence there was my first real exposure to any form of culture outside my own. It struck me as comforting in that it allowed me to reinvent my own identity. This would become a talent I perfected in this stage of my life and I used it to become whatever I was needed to be for whatever situation was at hand. Although I continued as a chameleon for the rest of my adult life, this particular skill did not go over well at school, and I soon found out what a paddle from the dean felt like. The move into California was also my introduction into your world for the first time and I did not understand it!

A year or so went by with little fanfare. I had been scolded for using curse language, experienced my first Christmas without snow, and had successfully gone one whole year without seeing a doctor for the first time in my life of eleven years. I also had become more involved in art. I entered contests at school and although I was never recognized, I was not ignored either.

Norma was becoming discontented and restless, so Johnny had requested a transfer to the desert. Originally our new place offered visions similar to where my uncle lived. When we arrived at the small town called Barstow, however, in the middle of the Mojave Desert, it was to find that the harshness of the life there was more extreme than anything I had every known, ever known existed. The people there appeared hardened, etched into the jeans they wore, with skin that told many tales. Trips to the ocean and the carnival parks became a thing of the past.

The little house sat on a dusty plat of land, ten acres in size, at the end

of a road surrounded by sagebrush. Walls of hot dust, rocks that

glimmered in the daytime, crooked telephone poles that dangled glass

beads and strings of copper, peppered the landscape. I used to stare at

those lines, imagining they led to treasures on the other end. The only reference point I had to my previous home was the water hole I found in the middle of a field that otherwise served as a yard of rocks. As we pulled up to the lone stretch of slightly paved dirt road, a man came to greet us with a smile.

"Hello thar', par'ner. Welcome!" The man in rigid jeans that hovered somewhere above his gray boots, spoke loudly.

"Well, thanks. My family and I are moving in here today," Johnny replied.

"Would you like a hand?" offered the man.

This man became a friend to our family and worked our land as his own. I wish I remembered his name.

Some of my fondest memories come from this period of my life. Even though I had to learn new escape methods, the challenge made the experiences more attractive and exhilarating. By now, Norma had let me wear a regular shoe. I was finally twelve and able to put on a tennis shoe.

This allowed my right side to look like anyone else's. Even though I had no foot on my right side, we made up for it by stuffing socks and tissue paper in the toe of the shoe, and this made me feel as if I were getting a whole new start. With this trick of illusion, I could wear a boot, peddle a bike normally, and even drive someday! We were happy here, alone and distant as it was. We raised pheasants, chickens, and chuckers, or desert quails. We also had a couple German shepherds, Guy and Sarge. Sarge was a retired Marine Corps dog.

I remember how proud Johnny was of a horse we kept in the back corral we built. He bought the black Arabian stallion for Norma as a birthday gift and they called it Na'Ho. I learned how to drive, too, when Johnny bought an old '53 Dodge, a five-window truck. The floorboard was so rusted out we had to weld a kitchen chair to it just so I could sit up and drive. The only thing to hit was sagebrush, so the driving was easy. We learned how to use pistols, too, and we all thought Norma was cool in her gun holster.

One day, I had pissed off the drill instructor again. My punishment was to move a pile of wood into the back of a trailer so we could haul it away. After about ten boards or so, I uncovered a sidewinder rattler. I ran yelling inside the house and Johnny came out. He moved that entire pile from one spot to the next, but no snake. About five minutes later, I found it again and this time Mom came out with her gun to show off her newfound talent!

It was during this period I began to learn how to protect myself from the questions of others. The right clothes and the right haircut appeared to satisfy most people's inquiries into one's health. I learned quickly to never wear shorts. I had discovered the penalty for swimming in public long ago. To this day, my hair, shoes, and clothing remain the single point of focus for me every day that I am strong enough to groom or dress. I learned little secrets, including the one of stuffing my shoes with tissue or extra socks to appear as though I had a real foot filling the space. We had become cowhands of the high desert with the boots, jeans, and shaved haircuts to prove it. Even though I could not wear the boots for more than a few moments at a time, they did provide me with a glimpse into belonging. And all I ever wanted, all I ever attempted, was to belong.

Not too long after we'd moved into this wide-open range, Norma found a Soapbox Derby contest. When she asked if I would like to enter I said yes, being the brave little soul that I was. Johnny said he'd help me build a car. We were a lot poorer now and didn't have the wealth of tools or engineering skills we had in prior days, but boy did we have fun. I won an award, too, for the best dressed! The cars that raced passed and left me trolling behind at the starting gate were no match for my "Lil-Devil," a red and white, plywood boxed car that needed an extra push to slide down the hill.

I sure wished everyone I had left behind could have been there.

We had access to the extended military stables in the area and once rode horses out to a place called Calico Ghost Town. I always was quick to let my alligator mouth override my hummingbird ass, and this day was no exception. Mom always rode a fast pony and today I asked her if I could ride hers and she could ride mine. Well, all four feet two inches of me climbed aboard with the confidence of a fool. We were about ten minutes into the ride, sitting at the entrance of a long stretch of abandoned road when Johnny asked me if I thought I could handle a "little run."

"Yaha!" I shouted, not waiting for the word, and took off, my legs barely able to hold onto a bicycle, let alone a fifteen hundred-pound horse in full gallop.

Within seconds, Johnny and another man were alongside me, attempting to grasp onto the reins of the excited horse, shouting "Don't let go, Kris, *don't let go!*"

My body was now bouncing on the saddle, its horn the only thing I had to hold onto to keep me on the back of the horse. Each second was an hour and the road ahead was becoming treacherous due to the chunks of abandoned asphalt. Each stride of the massive animal made me feel I had landed on a trampoline of rubber tires.

I noticed out the corner of my eyes, which I am sure were the size of grapefruits, that two men were reaching from either side for the charger's head to steer him down from the run. I heard the swoosh of a hoof racing past my head as I let go of the horn. Instantly I was tumbling like a rag in a washing machine, scraping, sliding, and slicing across the "road." My arms and knees burning on impact, it appeared that my previous twelve years of pain management was coming in handy. Norma, in full run and screaming, moved to catch me, and was met with a bloody, but laughing, teenager-in-the-making. "Kris, are you okay? My God, look at you!"

"I think so, Mom. But believe me, I won't do that again." I was feeling pretty good, actually, thinking the ride had come to a satisfyingly safe finish.

"Damn right, you won't!" said the ruffled a voice I had come to know too well. "Get your ass on that horse, boy!" said Johnny. "We aren't done just because you wouldn't listen. ...You just had to ride that horse...."

Norma turned over the reins of my original slow horse to me with a scolding smile and I finished the ride home with a smile of my own.

We also traveled a lot. We piled into our old International pickup or Rambler station wagon for trips across country, stopping along the road to camp, hunt, and fish in the wide-open spaces of the western landscape. I had a new beagle puppy after our German shepherds had passed on; Scooter was his name. I also learned how to clean and feather a host of birds real fast after a band of coyotes attacked one night.

On the Colorado River just outside Needles, our campsite was often a happy place. The heat waves danced across the water as the fire burned long into the night. The purple majestic ambers slowly gave way to a gold shine of darkness, the likes of which I have never seen since. Perhaps these are the memories that continue to drive me towards the water's edge as an adult.

I learned a lot about life in those years, but still never felt part of the

rest of the world in any given situation. Perhaps the isolation of the desert

does that to a person, too, allows them to disappear without explanation.

It's a place where the elements strip the flesh from anything not able to

fight the battle. I fought, but never could win that fight. And though I have

many times wished for a second chance to combat the wrongs of my life, I

have only been able to do the best I could with what I was given.

Johnny retired from the Marine Corps a year or so later in a grand ceremony. For me it was astonishing to see him in that context. I don't think I ever let him know that I was proud of him. I was too busy blaming him.

My Mom was working for a water company in Hinkley, keeping books and all. It seemed like everyone knew everyone in those days, and people were all to glad to help you when you needed or asked. I went back once to visit that little town many years later to find our tiny farm. The stalls were long since gone, of course, dry walls of dust the only thing still standing.

We were soon to leave the great state of California; it was 1973. We had seen all the glory of thousands of miles, mountains that shined, waters that talked. Each journey was eclipsed only by the visual discoveries around the next corner, and sometimes we didn't see another person for days. The time was set for us to embark on our last trip across country in our old truck with a camper. A '66 thunderbird in tow, we slowly moved over the crest onto the plains of Middle America to rejoin the family we had left behind in Indiana.

There were temporarily distractions with visits to places that echoed of carnival rides and street-fair barkers. Mom and Johnny often went to Las Vegas for a day trip or an evening of fun and took me with them. I enjoyed these trips immensely and the sights in those days were risqué even by today's standards. Women with enchanting smiles and clothes of rainbows. Men enthralled by the lights that led to dens of unspoken pleasures. Utopia, I suppose, of a sort that promised love for the common man. I spent most of my time at the Circus Circus; it was there I felt the connection to a fabric deeply woven into my own history. The excitement, mystery, and intrigue were beguiling, and I felt at home. I was not particularly interested in gambling, but being there was like the movies into which I escaped every chance I got. I treasured the experience of going to the theater, which I did regularly; there, for that brief time, nobody could see me. I was released to be someone else, to have another identity. The characters on the screen spoke to me without judgment and demanded nothing of me.

We traveled across a vast sea of grass. Dodging between thunderstorms, cooking lunch from the catch, our miles became a classroom of experiences never repeated. Our windows were like a television that rolled through programs of nature, each one offering a new scene with fresh smells that spoke of the land we traveled. Strangers slid past our view and with each mile became another memory.

In reflection, our life was the journey of misfits. We were actors reading a script lost long ago. And after many nights, which all became dawns, the masquerade slowly ended.

143

Chapter 12

A SHORT STAY

The rackety clanks and squeaks of the long journey ended; I sat up with great anticipation to see what would appear around the corner of the tree-lined gravel path ahead. Our arrival had been timed to the reunion and inaugural opening of a little hand-built cabin in the woods found at the end of a trail. I would attend my first six months of high school while living there, once again transplanted into a new location, house, and life.

Trail's End

"In the peace of the wood
Nature's made it her task to make one tranquil place
where in harmony I bask.

My small piece of heaven
where my cares can all mend
I am happy contented
here at Trail's End.

It seemed like forever
I searched, couldn't find
One spot on the earth,
Where I found peace of mind.

Now I've found it, I'm happy
And you're welcome, my friend
If you're seeking contentment
It is here at Trail's End.

Come sometime in autumn
See the wild colors blend,
Or come in the spring-time
It's so nice at Trail's End

It's so great a sensation
When I come around the bend
To know I'm back in my own world
Here at home, at Trail's End."
Johnny, August 1973

The reunion was a blast that year in the rugged three-room cabin.

Dogwood trees lined the back, which opened to a pole barn that kept J.

P.'s equipment and woodworking tools safe from the cold winter soon to

arrive. Although we were still many months away from December, the

cool mornings of the September school-bus rides and the questions asked

a hundred times were just weeks away. Living with my Grandma and

Grandpa was a great experience for me, but challenging for them, I'm

sure. Daily conversations had to be had surrounding my health and capacities. With a clear limp and lack of mobility, I was not about to join the football team or take part in anything that required physical aptitude.

When winter came, Mom joined Johnny on a cold snowy day to move into a house with old wood floors and noisy doors just down the street from the three-room house where they had been married in Muncie. I was enrolled in yet another school, attending one without ever finishing the last, a trend which would continue throughout my life.

That was the pattern of life we lived nowadays: move here, stay there. Our lives begin to revolve around alcohol, more and more with each passing year. Johnny grew to resent my mother's request for him to retire from the service, although secretly I believed he too resented the Corps for stealing his life away. Only those who have experienced that life know what it does. At thirteen, I found myself involved with several kids who liked to smoke dope. Considering I was the blond-haired kid from California in a group of kids who'd never left the city, I underwent another transformation to fit in. I never really knew which direction to go, how to belong. I always knew that I would never be equal to the rest.

Nevertheless, given a good lie, a little courage from that bottle of schnapps we paid for with our allowances, I was as strong or able as the complete people were. I had discovered an equalizer. Unable to appreciate the way it had affected the lives of those before me and the destruction it wrought, I thought only of the oblivion and the transformation it lent. As long as I did not look into a mirror, I was good to go.

Perhaps it was exactly at this stage of my life that Norma abandoned her attempts to discipline me. The new lack of guidelines allowed me the freedom of expression I thought I wanted, but I am more tempted to think that she was too tired to try anymore. Our lives were full of those great stabs at life, the ones where everyone sobered up long enough to take a trip to the cabin, go fishing perhaps. Then the stress of paying the monthly bills, losing another job, and the need to move again would release the ugly valve of indulgence. For a while, there was always another geographical cure.

* * *

The year was 1974 and my hair was almost to my shoulders. I wore flannel shirts painted with graphics, my bellbottom pants stretching taller than my four-foot six-inch stature could hope to fit. I had been in nonrestrictive shoes for over two years now. My back began to show signs of altering its shape and I had started to lean to one side and walk with a pronounced limp.

Another surgery to straighten my arm failed, except for the lasting result of another scar to hide. I have never been able to use that arm because it has always been frozen at a ninety-degree angle, leaving me with limited extension. Over time, I discovered that since my body could not perform, my mouth and brain had to compensate. I never considered myself particularly intelligent, but Norma did the best she could with homeschooling whenever I was unable to attend public school.

I'd always heard that intelligence was an equalizer, so I assumed that meant I, too, could follow a path of higher thought. My chosen brand of equalizer offered more immediate results, however, though ultimately it did an even better job of detouring me from any idea of pursuing a formal education. Although I had above-average street smarts, it appeared I also

had few social skills, and only false courage to back up the ones I had. At

the time could still share a quick snip of humor, mostly at my own

expense, as well. Years later, however, I would be without a vein of

laughter to draw upon for my own salvation.

Chapter 13

ARMIDILLA TOWN & BACK

In the summer of 1975, in the area of Temple and Killeen, Texas there sat a trailer on a parcel of land that had the appearance of a home for lost souls searching for a fresh start. Unfortunately, that family was us, as we had once again moved in search of Johnny's personal identity, or perhaps to comfort Norma's need to be cared for. Either way, one of Johnny's other children from a previous marriage had since come to stay with us for a while. We had traveled that year after my last surgery, twenty of them by the time I was fifteen, and found ourselves in Little Rock, Arkansas. Coincidentally, J. P. and Hildreth also traveled south that year and we all delighted in the few weeks they were in close proximity. The town of Little Rock asked J. P. to ride in a parade aboard an old car with some fellow, a politician named Bill, whom I would later come to know by a different name. It was as predictable as the summer heat amid the haze of forest-green hills that J. P. would find his way to whatever party or parade was in the works.

Johnny had five kids by his previous marriage. Truth be told, I think my being insinuated into their brood was not a welcomed event. I can't say anything but good things about the overall experience that summer, though, because it was fun, filled with motorcycle rides and campfires. I believe it was around that time I began to figure out how I could offer to fix a beer or a glass of scotch for Mom that would allow me a sip of the evening. I can clearly see the bonfire with everyone sitting quietly as I watched for the next refill request. I quietly got stoned in transit. Who wouldn't want to let the cripple kid get the drink; give him something to do, right? I did not care; I was getting a chance to belong, escape, or disappear all in the same act.

I can remember one of Johnny's drunken episodes while we were still in Texas. Norma was ill on the couch, as she had been many times since we'd left California. Though living in the desert had sparked our lives with rich experiences, a cloud of pain had begun to envelop Norma's daily

151

affairs. At times, her now all too regular migraines were coupled by days of illness and discomfort. At that age I didn't know any different, and assumed they were part of that unknown world of "female conditions."

This time our trailer sat against a backdrop of dusty hills in the great Lone Star state, close to another military base. By now, Johnny's daily consumption was at least a case to my best guess. My stepbrother and I began to learn how to pick wild asparagus from the side of the road. Stealing the local farmer's vegetables led to quick getaways on a couple of rickety bicycles we'd found behind the barn of our rented can. Basically, we were nothing more than a couple of juveniles trying to find something to do.

With each week came another large box of Minute Rice that sat protected under the counter for me to use. Tonight's menu was special, the dish accented by a serving of green dandelions freshly picked that day. A chef I was not, but survival had forced me to learn to cook. I had already prepared another pan of rice with butter and salt on the stove when Johnny came into the room.

Norma made it a point to scrape Johnny's change from the bar each morning, noon, or night, after their forays into the gates of hell. The kitchen counter was littered with Schlitz beer cans, crushed and toppled against one another. The smell was that of a barroom, still soiled from the night before. Johnny was leaning to the side, one hand on his hip, his always-present soiled white Stetson on his head and half-opened plaid short-sleeved shirt displaying silver anchors of history. His jeans were turned at the cuff to reveal the same tattered, scuffed boots he'd been wearing for years. The dance began, loud drunken comments that amused only the fallen woman on the couch, and the attempt to avoid conflict at all cost.

Most nights when the jester appeared ready to wage war, I knew the correct steps to excuse myself and avoid the mental torture—and conflict—that was sure to follow if I didn't. Tonight would be different. I had to make sure my stepbrother not only had food, but would survive whatever was going to take place. As Johnny's anger surfaced, it was clear

I had to place myself between the two of them. In doing so, I became the target of something I had no capacity to control.

"It's your fault she's sick!" the man standing at the table's edge yelled.

Johnny moved closer, his words underscored with slam after slam of his fist on the table. I did not understand what he was saying—or why. The Marine Corps sergeant had fire emitting from his eyes, a demonic glint that made me step back. In a flash, he had encircled my neck with a length of wire and lifted me to the sink in a violent, but well-executed, maneuver. With all the effort the dying can command, Norma rose to her feet and demanded Johnny put me down.

"Put him down J. R., NOW!" she screamed, holding her abdomen. She hobbled into the kitchen. My stepbrother was no fool and had silently disappeared into the other room.

I fell to the floor and waddled to the edge of the couch where my mother had been. In a moment, Johnny left the house in a fury. Rage had always gained results in our house and this time was no different...yet another skill I would later develop as a way to achieve the ends I wanted.

The following morning, I arrived at Indianapolis International to be greeted by my dad, Don Jr. Perhaps he was glad to see me, I don't know, but Don was polite and quick to take on the role I needed at the time. I always knew my Dad to express love through money—it was all about the size of the next gift. I believe now that his efforts were based on the fact that he'd never had financial security himself growing up and he simply wished to do better.

At the start of school in 1975, I was considered a misfit by appearance and, now, because of my antisocial behavior. Not being able to care for me since he was a bachelor, Don asked, or perhaps imposed on, Flossie, the one true stable person in our lives. Flossie's husband had passed on and the hope was she might be good for a boy who obviously was not adapting to society as well as expected. I did not deserve Flossie's grace and kindness; I only wish that I had appreciated the efforts she made on my behalf and her for making them.

155

I was like a kid in a candy shop, the jars overflowing. I was going to another new school where nobody knew me again and Grandma was fixing me dinner every night. Norma had stayed in Arkansas and would not be around for a while. I felt that it would be a period of rest for her, one she deserved. I was well aware of the burden I had caused, the liability I had become.

Don bought me the first in a series of cars. It was a 1961 Oldsmobile F85 with a pushbutton gearshift, and needed oil top-offs daily. I parked it on the street because Flossie did not want oil stains on her driveway. Soon that car was replaced with a '64 Buick convertible. I loved that car. I learned how to kiss a special young woman in the front seat, and had my first glimpse of a pair of breasts in the back. I was naïve, amazed that anyone, especially this beautiful girl I had come to know, would allow me to touch her. How could she involve herself with me, in my twisted and ugly state of existence?

My feathered wavy hair and blue eyes held some weight, but I was never going to be like the others. Always aware of what people saw when

156

they approached me, I stuck my hands in my pockets and wondered how badly my limp would put them off. Always hoping to avoid the inquiries, my mask was never enough.

There were the usual questions, this time from the girl in my car. "What happened?"

I answered methodically, attempting nonchalance, "I was born this way. It's the way God wanted it."

I really did see myself that way, and still do. I have lived my life with that vision of reality. The girl's questions were quickly replaced by a second, not-as-awkward kiss; I wanted to make sure I would develop my skills in that area into a talent. I lost my virginity to that precious young woman the same night we saw the movie MASH. Was it possible I belonged after all?

No longer a virgin, running around with a neighbor kid whose dad was a cop, supplied with pocket money when I asked for it, and a convertible! What else did I need? Oh yeah, a guy down the street who bought us punk kids booze because he knew one of us was a cop's kid. We drank enough schnapps, Heineken, and tequila sunrises to float a high school. In fact, I think that's what we were trying to do. We were the suppliers that year for booze before all the big events—the prom, the county fair, the local games. The one difference among us was that I never drank like the rest of the people around me, even then. I measured out what they needed against what I wanted. And by then I wanted whatever I could get.

Alcohol served a social purpose for the others, and allowed them to be funnier or kinder or more generous—sometimes towards me. Some of them appeared more intelligent...or did it only seem that way to me? It seemed from the start that mood-altering chemicals were destined to be a part of my life. The people around me must have been concerned about my consumption, but no one ever asked, "Kris, do you think you have a problem?"

Was it because they expected no less from the crooked image standing in front of them? Was it because our family gatherings included the most regular guest of all—alcohol? Either way, I never saw the same level of abuse and aggressive use I would later experience in my own life. Was it nature or nurture that led to my thirst to escape into chemicals? Were my addictions due to the host of needs and wants that would never be filled? I don't know, but an invalid at forty, cast aside by a society of winners and success stories, I know I have lived my life rummaging for an existence that could never be found.

In high school, on the "good side" of town, I felt even more out of place. I felt exposed. The braces and corrective shoes were gone, though I still needed them. Experiencing puberty like any other "normal" teenager was disconcerting to say the least. How could I grow into a normal teenager when there was nothing normal about me to start with? I began a steady retreat by means of an egotistical shell that kept me isolated from the overtures of others. My bearing was grandiose, loud, and emotionally underdeveloped.

I had no real avenue for stopping this progress. I expanded my horizons in the only way I knew how—in my dreams of leaving the town where I felt so trapped. Another geographical cure would fix things, surely. The problem was I had no way or money to do it. I had no skills and was extremely restricted physically. Since I'd gotten back from California, I had become aware of the limits, pain, and discomfort related to arthritis which occurred with the cold and wet weather. Norma's migraines had passed to me as well. Although most of my headaches related to my skeletal problems, it seemed they also appeared from stress.

I had tried a couple of regular jobs by now, washing dishes, flipping burgers, and the like. Every time I was let go or fired. I lived my life with the understanding that each time I had been given a chance because my dad or some family member had stepped in to aid my efforts. I had also adopted an attitude of reversed dependency that would not serve me well in the years to come. Either way, I still could not carry a large box and was less quick and less strong than even the weakest able body next to me. I had learned shortcuts and tricks to complete the tasks I needed to accomplish, but that is all they were, tricks.

While staying with Flossie, I involved myself with a community theater group and discovered that I could also change my identity through acting.

160

My artwork, what little painting I had done so far, was amateur at best. The need to leave reality behind was gaining more strength everyday. I auditioned for the local *Wizard of OZ* production on a cool fall day. I hoped to be considered for the role of a masked munchkin, but dreamed of a grander part.

I was home when the phone rang. "I'll get it, Grandma! Hello, Cross residence. ...REALLY?! Yes, Ma'am, I'll be there!" Unbelievably, I had the part I had hoped for...the best, the first, the wizard!

I spent the next few weeks preparing, fine-tuning my life's purpose. This must have been one of the few proud moments for my family. The work involved did not hurt me or involve physical constraints beyond my abilities. I could do it! I would succeed solely on my own.

Everyone was present every one of the seven nights we preformed. I was the wizard with blue hair, sprayed into a frenzied mess, and a robe of garments heavier than I was. A heavy paper-maché mask finished off the costume. In this world of fantasy I became someone else, someone who

161

never once harmed, explained, or scared another person. My antics brought laughter, joy, and thunderous applause. I think if I had sat in the audience I too would have been astonished that the deformed child was playing the part of the great wizard.

This would be my highest achievement in life; I was the wizard, which is how it was supposed to be! The feeling of exhilaration could not be beat. I spent many other months searching for it in other plays. I had many other supporting parts, but never again a lead role. My acting experiences took on the same pattern I experienced when drinking or using drugs, that of searching for a high point of oblivion. I had started my journey of riding the rollercoaster, from extreme highs to bottomed-out lows.

But, man, didn't that breeze feel good.

* * *

I started to research New York in hopes of finding a place to belong. It was just before high-school graduation when Norma convinced me not to aim for that challenge. I had prepared roughly twenty-five letters to various families in the region to ask if they would extend their kindness to allow me room and board while I explored my acting possibilities. I will never know if Norma's advice was the best, but it was the safest, and that was her job as she saw it: to protect her son as best as she could. I never went to New York, and I never acted again.

Perhaps the curtain might have closed on our lives at that point and been more than enough. But with each disappointment only the faces changed. By now Norma had a perpetually tired appearance that weighed heavily on all of us who saw it. I alone knew and accepted the reason behind it.

Chapter 14

THE COLD TRIP

Lying in bed with the chill of a winter's breath in the small house, I dreamed of what I could do to make myself a man. Flossie had graced me with far more care than I deserved. There's that word again, the reminder that I would never believe myself deserving, no matter what came my way. The smell of cigarettes followed me from the bedroom into the kitchen, where I found this angel of a matriarch sitting at the same place where she sat everyday, eating her breakfast. Her life was so clean, and rewarding her with my ignorance was something I felt I could no longer do.

"Grandma, I think I'm going to go visit Aunt Charlotte and Uncle Fred in Logansport today," I said with purpose in my voice.

It was January 22, 1978. Graduation last year had come and gone with little meaning for me, though it seemed to have importance to those around me, at least according to the pictures. Only Norma knew that due to all the time spent traveling and the lack of appropriate documentation I had been unable to receive a diploma. It was through sheer intimidation, or by conjuring a sympathy vote, that Norma had convinced the school administrators to allow me to limp-walk across the stage during the ceremony. I disguised that fact through lies for many years. Once again, it appeared I was a less-than-engaging player. Time for a move...

After my statement to Flossie, I packed away a few belongings in a small duffel bag, I felt energized and scared all at the same time. My fear of inadequacy had followed me all my life. I knew that should I become lost in my active escape with alcohol and drugs I would not be able to find my way home. But, with one last kiss and hug, I left my refuge and began to drive.

With a quick stop at the local town drunks' house to gain a little courage and some herbs to use along the way, I was off on my first journey alone. Being alone was not a new feeling, but the need to find a new home by myself was. It was a cold drive and the car's exhaust roared loudly. My '66 Chevy took me deep into Indiana farm country. The houses appeared like dots and then grew with each beat of the music that hid the sound of the rattling windows. Trees, showing signs of better days, lined the roads, like dead spectators of time or protectors of the future.

My mind filled with the illusion of hope that perhaps where I was going people would see me as a different type of man or that I could become the kind of person I so clung to in my fantasies. Each rush of the wind against the car shook the body but I plowed my way along—foolish, young, and drunk.

Logansport appeared lost in time, with railcars pushed and piled into a formation next to the grain elevators. The sedans looked older and fewer than in the world I had just left. My journey took me down to a level lower than the rest of the countryside. I felt the depression that extended beyond the physical sights to the people themselves, who seemed to be walking aimlessly about. Shocked and saddened by the reality, my expectations evaporating in front of my eyes, I kept on towards my destination.

The familiar Plymouths that so often arrived in Gnaw-bone on August afternoons sat in front of the house. I knew that this was the home of a warm reception. I knocked on the door and with a burst of enthusiasm Charlotte grabbed me, pulled me into the warm room, heated by the steel box in the corner, and said, "My God, it's Norma's boy, Kris. Fred, come here!" Charlotte still spoke in the same high-pitched gasp I remembered so well.

"Well, look who's here, how are you, son?"

I guess I have to say that if you don't have an Uncle Fred in your family, I hope you find one. Uncle Fred's unconditional love encircled those in his presence, and was selfless, his soft heart worn on his sleeve for all to witness. If you needed anything he had, it was yours with no questions asked. His dedication to his ill-fated wife and children had left him a simple man with simple means. Paradoxically, he had become the most respected member of our entire family. I always loved this man.

"I'm doing great, Uncle Fred, Aunt Charlotte. I wanted to take you up on your offer, visit for a while, if I might." I didn't remind them that this was an invitation from years ago.

Fred responded with the belly laugh that came from his round and solid, stocky frame, "Sure you can! Get this boy something to eat, Maw. He's hungry from that long drive." My aunt was eager to serve, complaining all the way. She'd lie down in front of a bus for you, but yell the whole time about how much you'd better appreciate it.

Uncle Fred's chair, grooved into the wood floor that squeaked from years of neglect, was quickly filled again as he watched the football game I had interrupted. Soon my grilled-cheese sandwich and soup, the substance of many meals to come, was on the table.

Not long after I finished, my cousin Billy, with whom I'd always had great fun at family reunions, arrived to say hello and welcome me to his territory. His sister Jenny, also warm and sincere, was in tow. I felt accepted and said a prayer that maybe this was going to work out after all.

Perhaps this next stab at life was the one that could align my actions with my soul and provide me with a reason for my distorted and deformed consciousness.

After a good night's rest, a few secretively shared joints, and a couple of public beers with my newfound family we stared at the television on that dried-out wood floor. The voice on the television was repeating the word "blizzard" over and over. With northern Indiana securely positioned in snow country, blizzards were not unusual in the spectrum of winter experiences.

Although there was plenty in the food pantry, we needed to prepare for the worst by collecting firewood and making sure everything was in order. I was as busy as could be trying to adjust my knowledge of the big city to this small collection of nonconformists in the middle of corn silos. Our preparation lasted well into the night, radios positioned next to flashlights, waiting and ready for what might come.

For the next two days we were confined to the small saltbox house. Next door was a building Fred owned as well, which served as the spot for drugs, music, sex, and booze. After all, it was the '70s and there was nothing else to do, right? The weather precluded any outdoor activities on this cold day so, with an introduction to a few neighborhood teenagers and some of my fine big-city herb, I was allowed to be a part of another crowd of shadows.

Five or six days went by before the sound of traffic replaced the snowy hush and the cardinal's song. The slush rose above the snow angels we had created. As the sun bounced brightly off the surfaces, my head throbbed from pain brought on by the partying of the day or night before. Shoveling snow was quickly replaced by foolish affairs and the behavior of hoodlums on the loose. Glory had arrived in this newfound group of misfits, a spot where I appeared to belong.

The woman with whom I had been having sex for the past week was simple in her enjoyment of being lost in smoke-filled rooms with strangers who took her body for pleasure. The cousins I had known only slightly when we had mischievously snuck drinks at Trail's End took on the traits of gangsters with a lust for oblivion. The gift of a simplified life and the stability of a loving matriarch only appeared to encourage us to rage with more insanity.

Then the phrase "perfect storm" didn't exist, but our antics had all the content and character of a blizzard and tornado combined...active and violent delusion coupled with mind-altering chemicals and the reckless abandon for personal gluttony. If there was a God besides the plastic Jesus hanging on the kitchen wall of the saltbox, I did not care nor want to know.

Realizing my need to make a living, I used my blond-hair-and-blue-eyes trick to secure a job at the local mall to sell shoes. Yes, shoes! How ironic, the three-fingered, good-looking freak who had no toes and no feet, selling shoes. I made it a point to once again separate from what I was in order to become what I wanted.

The idea that I had been given another opportunity excited me enough to allow the second act to continue. Dressed up in a suit Fred bought for me for my new job, I looked distinguished, like somebody who had direction. The new kid in town, I regularly ate alone at a local pizza place. With my capacity to manipulate any given situation by taking advantage of peoples' kindness or sympathy, I soon met a peculiarly talkative waitress. But this one was different, more like me! I guess it was the fact that she talked to me as though I was a person.

In a nutshell, Logansport had twenty-five thousand people, twenty-seven taverns, seven whorehouses (run by the Police Chief and Mayor), two strip clubs, two biker gangs, a train station, and a state mental hospital—most of whose patients had been released into the community. Captured in time or in a parallel universe that only discloses itself when you appear above the sinkhole, Logansport was a place not entirely visible to the outside world.

But back to the waitress who didn't treat me like a freak. "I notice you never eat with anyone," she said one day in a smart-ass tone, her inflated chest pointed in my direction.

"Well, if you must know, I'm new in town," I said. "By the way, I like the way you pour beer. You're kinda strange too, aren't you?"

The three hundred-pound thin-haired woman, whom I later came to know as Annie, reared up as if to strike out at me. But then something made her reconsider. "Well, I can see right now that I like you, kid!" she said in a cigarette-callused voice. "I'm having a party this Friday, you want to come?"

Of course I did, I told her, and watched as she walked away with as much attitude as she had when she appeared. It was not that I had never been invited to a party. But when you party, you can spot another partier from a mile away. I guess that ability crosses the discrimination line to unite drunks and fools.

I grew to like this woman, Annie. We grew together and then apart eventually, probably because we were more alike than different. I still wonder how she fared. She, too, had had her cards dealt from the bottom of the deck.

A few days later, I appeared at her party, looking for all I was worth as a child of the '60s. A pair of pink, yes, pink, nylon pants. Three-inch platform shoes; a silver silk winged-collar shirt trimmed in purple, unbuttoned mid-chest for vanity's sake. In addition, I sported a corduroy hat that tilted slightly to the right, and a pair of mirrored sunglasses. My hair rested on my shoulders. All five feet of me knocked on the door. Since nobody knew me and I was new to town, image was everything.

I knew how to be cool. I stood in the corner and watched everyone with that cool eye of judgment and conceit, smoking a fine bit of herb. At one point a woman who seemed more mature than the others came up to me in that corner, reached out, took my pleasure from my crippled fingers, and encircled her lips around the joint at the very place mine had just been and I was in ecstasy in one fell swoop.

Chapter 15

EIGHTEEN YEARS OVER

A rush of drug-induced activity swallowed my imagination as I began
to live and breathe the grown-up world of the '70s drug culture. The fact
that Gail, this woman I had met at a party, had become pregnant mattered
little in my daily life. I was free to do as I wished; I was a man! In fact,
errant egotistical boy with an inferiority complex might have described me
better over the next few years. In these days I worshipped themes
expressed by Bob Seeger, BTO, Rush, and Boston to complement the
quaalude acid sounds of Pink Floyd, Aerosmith, Black Sabbath, Zeppelin,
and Head East.

My previous experience providing the local children with cocktails in
my hometown quickly secured me in a position of distributor in my new
terrain. As I began to mingle with Gail's brother Kyle and the other active
party-scene goers, I fell into a promotional slot that filled both my mind
and pockets.

Cannabinol Tea, Columbian Gold, Panama Red, Thai Stick, Tuenols, with a glass of wine or a Tom Collins or rum on the balcony: I had it all. On a typical summer day, you could find me lingering about the balcony, smoking the best herb to be found that particular week and chatting to the passersby. At seventy dollars a quarter pound, I sold three to make a profit of one for me. Monthly trips to Chicago's Southside only added to the flavor of mixtures available to those of us who kept close to our circle of friends. Since my new roommate was unable to drink or partake of the pleasures anymore, I insanely took in enough for the two of us.

By now, my reputation as dealer and life of the party had preceded me into the center of town, preventing me from securing a real job. My capacity to support a family was nil and my active addiction had exploded. Sitting in a collection of fools one night high on purple microdot acid, my new nickname became Kris Kringle.

Conveniently excusing ourselves from what others judged as "normal," a few of us similar in attitude began to run together. Hollywood, Niger-Mac, and Crazy George were among our group. Hollywood (Kenny) used to announce his philosophy, "I live fast and hard and I'm gonna die fast and hard!" he'd say. "In fact," the polished-looking man of twenty-eight continued with bravado, "I'll die before my thirtieth birthday!"

We cringed at this deceleration because it likely meant at least one more of us would end up a statistic as well. Although I was a lot younger than Hollywood, I admit I held the same belief.

Norma had kept a close eye on me during this time. Between her and Aunt Charlotte, they had devised a plan to transfer J. P.'s mobile home to a small clean back lot on the outskirts of town. During one of their random visits, Johnny and my mother announced they were moving in down the street. I was oblivious to what must have been a heart-wrenching sight for my mother—me at my most drunken, slovenly worst.

If we're lucky we have people in our lives on whom we can depend. I had my mother. I hope that my dependence on her was healthy. I had tried to adjust to the fact that I had become an embarrassment to her, but by now, my behavior was unchecked and extreme. With no rules to follow

177

and little, if any, respect for the people around me, I lost sight of the values with which I had been raised. With a grandchild on the way, Norma did not hesitate, however. Convinced the right thing to do was have me marry the mother of my child, Norma plunged herself into the affair of planning my wedding. Gail's family, on the other hand, found little to celebrate in their daughter's choice of a fallen man determined to do nothing but dissolve their daughter's life.

Gail was more of a codependent by association. This was a position she knew well from rehearsing it with her own father. Kyle Senior was a strong figure of a man—when sober. Unfortunately, no one knew him sober any more—nor did they want to, for he was too much fun drunk. Oh, how this group of strangers fit together seamlessly, each placed into position without force or complaint.

Surprisingly, the formal evening of our wedding went off as planned. All those who had spent time at the family cabin came to drink the warm, whisky Christmas-dinner cocktails and enjoy an evening of laughter. They all came, snapping pictures of the sorrow of a pregnant bride, the fool of a groom, and lost integrity.

Each whispered to the next the secret they shared and gossip filled the voids. "Well, at least the boy made it this far; maybe the girl can straighten him out." "I guess I would drink, too, but he acts an awful lot like his Grandpa!" "Hope that baby'll be okay? It would crush her—you know, Norma, that is. I don't think she could handle something like that again."

* * *

Indiana winters are harsh and in the year of 1979 it was no different. Life on 12th Street became as cold as the bitter chill of rain and snow that froze all life. Trapped by the lack of money and living solely on what little money Gail brought in working at the local hospital, I became more desperate. I was on a sure road to abject destruction, drinking for days now with no regard for the damages or consequences. Norma's anticipation was gaining steam and the toys, carriage, lace, and supplies had started to appear daily.

I found a talent that winter with which I had flirted before. At a local tavern, a gleeful bartender who served laughter with every drink had once invited me to play in a billiard game. I'd done pretty well and afterwards a man came up to me and introduced himself. "Would you like to learn how to play this game the way it's meant to be played?" he asked.

"I already know how to play," I said, cocky as ever.

The stocky, well-groomed man grinned and told me if I ever wanted to learn to let him know. I returned to a dirty table out front and drank, more concerned with oblivion than in learning something new.

A few more days wasted away. At one point I remembered my conversation with the grinning man. Having nothing to lose, I returned to ask him to show me what he meant. This man was quick to accept my curiosity, but also added that my drinking and drug use had to slow down if I wanted to absorb anything he had to offer. And so it started—my education in the etiquette of pool and how to take another man's money. I learned quickly how to respect another man's game, but identify his weakness. I paid attention to this man who was able to walk a round ball backwards or, against all odds, find the hidden shot. My mind fully engaged, I was soon playing in weekly games with more and more confidence.

I found a great pleasure in this simple assembly of ivories. Memories of the dirt floors in the Mojave surfaced, reminding me of another time when my body was able to perform in a way it otherwise would be denied. It felt freeing.

One Saturday night, my family watched me perform and emerge victorious. Was this actually something I was good at—was it possible that I might not be a freak after all? Later that winter I played a tournament game in which I won second place against the very man who had taught me. Although I was a winner that day, I fell victim to the same lure and mentality of the carnival, and would never again capture the glory of success. Instead, I became arrogant. I craved the hustle more than the pride of a game well-played. When I was lucky, I found the perfect pigeon. I always let him win the first game, let him feel the pride in beating me the first time…and then played the hustle the next time around. Always let them win the first one; that was the rule.

On some nights, after all the other part-time drunks had gone home, a group of us reopened the bar for our own amusement. The illusion of my acceptance kept me going back for more. On one such night, I found myself involved in a four-car accident just around the corner. Drunk and full of speed, which served only as a temporary filter for the rum of the day, I was lucky; the other three cars were parked against the curb when my car smashed into them. Only my first in a string of drunken auto accidents, it put an end to the '69 mustang.

I recall a certain police officer, one of the ones affiliated with the local department that ran the whorehouses, who came to my house to deliver my ticket. He seemed regretful. I sat smoking a bowl in my custom hookah as he negotiated a buy of samples for his own pleasure. "Sorry, Kris," he said, "but it's my job. I have to give this to you." Those were the days when your local Serve and Protect was involved in all phases of community service. In this little town, everyone got their fair share of servicing.

Whether it was attending a three-day hog roast with one of the two local biker gangs, spending the week traveling among the area taverns and strip joints to hustle pool, or selecting another sexual partner for me and others to share, my life had lost all semblance to the life of honesty in which I had been raised. I had my own child now, but rationalized that the child was the responsibility of the woman who had given birth to her. Why should I have to be burdened with a job or a child—or have any involvement in this fucked up world anyway!

In one memorable episode, I found myself at the same barstool as many other nights. I had eaten a peyote chip with a few other guys, looking for another turn at oblivion. Crazy George and Hollywood asked if I wanted to go out to Lake Circuit and dig in on a keg. Normally I'd jump at the chance, but for some unknown reason, I said no and decided to stay at the bar.

God has a mysterious way of working sometimes. Later that night, on the way back from Lake Circuit, Hollywood was traveling over 120 MPH. According to the report, as the tires of the car sped towards the ravine, sliding and rolling along the pavement, George's leg became caught between the roof and the window. Kenny was ejected from the car, which then landed on top of him and crushed his chest. He survived long enough for George to hear his friend's last gasp, the blood of both men staining the car's white interior. The lights had gone out for the man who had predicted his own death just weeks short of his thirtieth birthday, and months short of the birth of his child.

* * *

Insanity as a description of my life sat comfortably, leaving little doubt for all factions of what I had become. Despite my best intention of settling down, my episodes of destruction brought about only more devastating outcomes...destroying furniture, throwing items about in fits of rage, blacking out. I never remembered what I had done, and even found perverse glee in the tales of what I had done the night before. This torture had to end. I knew that. But how?

The spring of 1980 arrived after a number of wasted months. As usual, my participation in life was clouded by the current drug or that week's flavor of schnapps. Soon it was evident that I had no ability to support, or even partly guide, my family. I found myself sitting at the table in the dark for hours, either drunk or sketching drawings that resembled ancient warriors. Soon people around me were requesting more extravagant poster-sized paintings, and drawings of their cats or dogs to display. I found that even in my delusional state I could produce a rough surreal art form that had a market value, enough to supply funds for increased chemical escape.

Through all of this was the ongoing relationship that Norma had developed with her granddaughter. The two of them had the kind of magical connection that all children seem to have with their grandparents. Norma was proud to spend time with her, entertaining her and encouraging laughter and joy. Flossie and Hildreth added to the mix with more love and adornment. Flossie, in her talent for clothing, created a coat made for picture-perfect winters at the cabin.

With the following summer came the Indiana heat, scorching our little apartment. Norma, disappointed and embarrassed by my lifestyle, had left town with Johnny to return home, leaving their trailer available for the three of us to occupy. Norma had realized that her presence was not going to change my spiraling decent.

In August, Gail and I learned that her father, Kyle Sr., had begun working in Houston, Texas. Rumors of a job boom in an otherwise depressed economy had made their way up North. Never one to refuse a road trip, I grabbed my belongings and sped down to join the rush.

When I arrived, I found myself initiated into a club of four men whose lives were dedicated to substance abuse. This time, my wife's father was the conductor. We lived in a fine suburban home and cashed our weekly checks to stock the bar with the best liquor we could afford. Women were revolving ornaments in our clamoring for booze and the money with which to buy it.

On one occasion, we had included a woman and her husbands' credit cards and Cadillac in our debauchery. We woke on Sunday morning to discover her gone and the cupboards left bare. Among the five of us, each with incomes of two thousand a week, we managed to collect enough money to track down a bag of Mexican Ragweed and seven bottles of Thunderbird wine in time to watch football for the day. Not surprisingly, our welcome in this five-bedroom home in an upscale neighborhood ended shortly thereafter. Evicted, we scattered like rats into the city. We were connected through marriage, but Kyle had no real need or desire to drag me along when he left, so we parted ways.

A drinking acquaintance from Logansport had since come down to get in on the work boom. The two of us collected our meager belongings and packed them into the crippled car I had driven to Texas. I had learned a lot from Johnny, and had never been afraid of doing what I needed to do to survive, so the transition from luxury to a local truck stop became the solution. We worked all day in local factories and spent the cold nights parked between the rigs. One afternoon, I returned "home" from work. I searched the truck stop, not believing my eyes. One of the servers came over. "Are you Kris?" she asked.

"Yeah, I was trying to find my friend," I said, denying what I already knew I'd hear.

"Yeah, well, that's what I need to tell you," she said. "He left some stuff here behind the counter and took off. Sorry."

My "friend" had stolen most of my belongings. Defeated, I washed up inside the washroom at the truck stop. The next day I was fired because I brought vodka with me to the job.

Incredibly, I was still capable of selling my potential. Sobering up long enough to gain a secure job with another company the next week, I applied for immediate housing on a bus line. That's how I found myself living on a floor with cockroaches as my companions.

The days passed. Evenings of loneliness and despair made me wish for home. I had reached the end of my thirty-day probation period at work and had shown only my inability to perform the work I had promised. The regular watchful eye of authority soon recognized my poor attendance record and my lack of sobriety. A week before Christmas, I was dismissed for my lack of character. Or was it my attitude...or my hopeless state of mind...or my social inadequacy?

I called Don and asked him to please, fly me home; I needed help and couldn't do it anymore. Once again I was rescued from Texas, except this time my downfall had been entirely my own doing. I spent the next couple of days shopping for Christmas gifts in downtown Houston, wearing the brown dress suit I had brought to impress people I would never see again.

I recall the moment when I arrived at the airport in Indianapolis. I had developed a knack by now for behaving foolishly at just the wrong time. In my straw cowpoke hat complete with rooster feathers, blue jeans and a Texan flannel shirt, I likely appeared to my father as a king's jester. I walked towards him, standing tall, crisply dressed, with the Barbie of the week on his arm. I could see in his eyes his dislike for my appearance—probably for me. I had a firm understanding of what that look said.

I returned down into the belly of the town I had left so easily. I greeted my family with cautious excitement. You could have cut the tension with a blade of grass. Who is he now? What did he do while he was gone? Can he support a family? Did he grow up? When will the next drunk or blackout happen? None of these questions would go unanswered for long. Enthusiasm was quickly replaced with arguments and frustration. My alcoholism was clearly past the point of no return, a physical and mental obsession that did not intend to let go of me.

* * *

Years before I had attended an Alcoholics Anonymous meeting in a weak moment of desperation. I had gone to find an answer to my miserable existence and moral deformities. I left that experience with the resounding conclusion that I wasn't "that bad" yet—that I was nothing like everyone else there. Not me. Of course in hindsight, I had arrived at that stage of addiction long ago, when I was fourteen, stealing and drinking daily.

My return from Texas did not go well. My wife, for whom an angel's place in heaven resides, consulted with all the matriarchs of her life, including Norma, to cure my ailments. They decided that they would move me back to Muncie, to live under the same roof with Norma. They were hoping the new surroundings would instill in me some self-control—enough that I would get the education I needed. For some reason I was yet to understand, the players behind the scenes were set on orchestrating my life's affairs in their continued belief that supporting me was either a load to bear, or a cause worth the effort.

I found myself still alive, but wondered how anything positive, sincere, or holy could come from such a bedeviled life? It had gone unvalued by its owner for so long that one had to ask, Where was the hope? It has to be said that I had always noticed a crust of goodness outside myself; I just never felt I deserved to be included in it.

Many sacrifices were made on my behalf. Norma had placed all other happiness in her own life aside to contribute to mine, to raise her son. Through some circumstance, Johnny had returned to Arkansas to join the band of children he'd left behind. With Gail and Norma teaming up together, I was getting yet another stab at life. Surely this one would catch. Surely nobody could be that far gone, could have burned so many bridges he could not recognize the trail of broken hearts and dreams he was leaving in his wake?

Enrolled in the local technical college, I began classes to learn how to work in a society that distained me. I went grudgingly for the first few weeks to satisfy the need for proof of attendance and family scrutiny. The pull of the 300 Club, the Sportsman Bar, and Henderson's Tavern was too strong, though, calling me away with their pool tables, loose women, and cheap drinks.

Hence, no matter where I traveled, I never left. There I was, and thus, here I am.

Crushed and disappointed, Norma moved away and left my family treading water again. Needing an apartment, we lied and contrived our way into a duplex one block down from my favorite bar, which had the requisite five pool tables, plenty of working patrons needing to be entertained, and rum, plenty of rum.

Flossie appeared one day with a bag of food. Act Three in motion. I burned every dollar that came my way and continued what was now my age-old routine of opening the tavern at 6:30 in the morning. With the stench of bad breath and sweat from the night before, I drank tomato juice and a draught to cure my stomach. I sat next to whichever man needed to tell his tale to start his day; I became the jester for whoever was buying that morning. I knew how to be a jester. Then, as the marks began to appear, I hustled the tables for that day's fund.

The cycle repeated for months on end. Another Indiana winter had come and gone. I grabbed a job for a few weeks at a time, but never lasted long, always fearing they would discover my shortcomings, my failings. I made an art form out of selling them on my potential and disguising my limits—until I didn't.

Flossie checked on the child and comforted Gail when all seemed lost. Gail was traveling back to her hometown more frequently as we became more distanced. Her reaction to my drunk fool of a self was almost pure disgust by now. Not able to afford or manage sanity, my binges were a continuous effort to stay away…away from it all. I wanted die so badly that all I thought about was how, where, and when I could do it. It was no longer a question of if, simply of who would find my body and in what condition when I did it.

My attendance or lack thereof was no longer expected—or missed—at Christmas get-togethers. Since Norma had returned to be with her soul mate in Arkansas, I had no true kin who would listen to me, not that I could blame them. Gail had tolerated my rages, car crashes, and binges as long as she could. I was a complete embarrassment to the human race and showed no signs of considering anything other than complete, total humiliation.

Many nights I sat in a chair in the front room, drinking rum to kill myself in the most cowardly way possible. One night I rose from the chair and strolled into the kitchen. I then unzipped my pants and urinated in the vegetable drawer of the refrigerator. When I was done, I collapsed, passing out on the bed behind the door closest to me at the time.

Chapter 16

SURREAL SUMMER

My actions had reached the realm of abject insanity. They would have been better off sending me away. As it was, I had likely reached a point of no return.

Spring flowers and cool rainy days accented by the smell of raw dirt and the fishy aroma of worms dancing across the sidewalk filled the air. Through the veil of my alcoholic haze, I began to get the feeling that something was about to happen. Although I have never claimed to be a clairvoyant or even visionary, I have always known there is energy available to each of us, should we choose to use it. To use it wisely, however, has always been my dilemma. This time was different; I felt the need to wonder and look at the people around me. A change was coming. A change which stirred my soul.

I have learned that most functioning alcoholics and drug addicts have one characteristic in common: the knack of rising above their lives just enough to know that they do not have the capacity to cope with reality. Just enough common sense to support only that which will not interfere with their long-term plan to destroy themselves at a future point in time. This was the case for me now. Norma had not stopped coming to Indiana, sometimes with Johnny, to see us. My daughter was a magnet for her and the two of them were alike in looks and disposition. The need to be near her granddaughter gave Norma just enough of an excuse to check on her son.

This time I mustered up the ability to stay sober long enough to get drunk with Norma and Johnny in the spirit of celebration. My failings of the past months—and years—seemed to matter little. Norma looked as clear and beautiful as she had in at least ten years. With my best friend in the room, I paraded around as if to declare that my life was acceptable, progressing along without hitch. I was proud that I had recently taken another job and had actually gone to work for a couple of weeks. There was even a paycheck to spend on our celebration. Never mind the debt or overdue bills on the desk that Gail continually chased. My family had come to visit me; it was my duty to entertain them in the style they had come to expect. I only wish I could have offered the truth of my real emotions.

Many things went unsaid that day, but not necessarily unnoticed. We pretended that I wasn't lying, hiding what I did, thought, and felt. But I knew that Norma knew what was really going on. I did not have the wisdom or the courage, however, to talk to her about it. I also felt that Norma was not telling me everything. Sure enough, I found out later that her mother, Hildreth, was dying, and that she and Johnny had come to comfort J. P. and take care of what needed to be done in preparation for Hildreth's passing.

The following day we drove to the rest home where Hildreth had slipped away into a diabetic coma. In body, but not mind, I was able to call on some measure of strength to clean myself up in respect for my family.

Lying in fetal position, her eyes closed, I witnessed for the first time the

throes of death and experienced what I imagined it would feel like to

surrender to the silence. I was envious.

Saddened over the disintegration it imposed on my Grandfather, I felt a

certain resolve that it should not be the case that everything had to be this

hard. In fact, death would be comforting.

Norma and Charlotte, who also had arrived that day, would now jointly

take on Hildreth's role, filling a void her passing would leave behind for

the Parker family. At Hildreth's funeral, her soul was visible in all the

faces that skirted in front of us as they passed by her coffin. I had never

felt comfortable with the open display of the dead; nor did I agree with the

common practice of praising the dead simply because they were gone. To

me, it seemed altogether shallow and pointless.

As our family had so often done before, after the funeral we gathered

for a meal and to talk of earlier times. We talked of the cabin, the songs,

the laughter and joy of a simple path that had led to Trail's End. Soon afterwards, J. P. sold the cabin and folded his life into a small home next to the local golf club in town.

Our visit through these few days was predictable: party all day with food, drink, and music, usually ending up at a step-cousin's or uncle's house to enjoy each other's antics. Laughter and booze, card games of euchre, arguments of cheating, and the infamous family member passed out on the couch, one of the kids lying on top as if to secure the night. A Rockwell painting we were not. Capturing the heightened feelings of oblivion: a family trait. This time it was obvious that everyone was gravely aware of the absence of one of its most beloved members.

* * *

It didn't take long after Mom left that my feet were leaving a trail of footsteps to the door of my local watering hole again. I lost the job I'd been holding. And the hideous four horsemen—terror, bewilderment, frustration, and despair—haunted me day and night, as I continued to look for ways out of this hell on earth.

On one such day, shaking already at 6:00 in the morning, I watched my loyal companion shuffle the child out the door to a babysitter's before traveling to a job that she used as an escape from me. I somehow knew today would yield another blow. It wasn't but an hour or so later that J. P. called me to tell me that Norma had been taken to a hospital in Little Rock, to the local Air Force facility there. He went on to say that my mother had severe stomach pain and that the doctor had prescribed a medicine to resolve it. His call heightened my sense of my own mortality, but it also gave me the distinct feeling that something was going to happen that would change all of our lives forever. I knew it wasn't over yet.

Adding insult to injury in that little town of Logansport at the crevasse of a hill, Charlotte had fallen victim to the disease that had raped her mother. After the amputation of both legs and cognitive function was all but gone, Charlotte's heart and mind sent her into a stroke. She entered the realm of death a few weeks later. It was a painful escape without the blessing of silence. In a matter of only weeks, the Parker family had lost two of the only three pillars who supported it.

Oblivious to the extreme dissolution of our family, my efforts remained selfishly ignorant of the world about me. Why would I alter my direction simply because some of my elders had died? I was quick to use their deaths as an opportunity to garner sympathy, however. Sympathy was always good for at least a couple of extra drinks at the bar.

It was another Wednesday. They had begun to run together, rainy, sunny, cold, hot, *ad infinitum*. I wanted to disappear and the only way I could find to accomplish this so far was through filthy dirty alcohol and drug abuse. To hell with the family that sacrificed everything for me; they did this to me anyway. If it were not for them, I never would have been born and never have had this miserable life. Besides, my contribution to life and the parts of it that mattered did not exist! *Go to hell, world. Go to hell, God! You never did anything for me. You made me a freak, a joke. I wish to God I had never been born.*

Self-pitying and full of loathing, I cried in my beer. *I have the worst life in the world, how can I go on living like this?*

202

The phone rang loudly. With a familiar reticence to answer, I picked up the receiver. "Hello?"

"Kris." It was Don. "It's your mom. She has gone into surgery and you need to go to Arkansas."

A deep silence was the only response I had to offer.

Don went on. "I'll be there to pick you up in an hour. Take enough clothes to stay for a couple days—and for God's sake, son, be sober when I get there!"

I heard this demand clearly, even through the fog of alcohol.

I felt the urgency to move, but had no knowledge of what my place was. What role was I to perform?

As we drove to the airport, Don spoke to me only briefly and with a sharp cynicism about what I had become. His disapproval of his drunkard of a child was all too close to the disapproval he'd felt for his own father. It was a memory that continued to govern his own actions, how he too would use emotional detachment as an escape from the news that had arrived that day.

He grasped my hand and put a packet of money into it with firm instructions. "Do not get drunk on this money, or I will beat you severely." He spoke with a hint of jest in his voice, but his eyes were serious.

We said our goodbyes, knowing the next stop on my journey would not be an easy one. I held back, not wanting to go. Nothing in my life had ever finished well, let alone begun well, and I sensed that this would not be any different. It would take all I had to summon the courage not to cry in front of Norma. It would take more willpower than I had to keep from accusing Johnny for her troubles. His wild life of trouble, his drinking and irresponsible lack of attention to family… How the hell could anyone do that to her?! Norma deserved better than him anyway… what a #$$%$#…; and so it went on inside my head and stayed.

The irony is obvious.

J. P. was already there, helping to manage Mom's care. I walked into a room with cold floor tiles. The bed was surrounded by a drawn curtain. Excusing herself, the nurse stepped aside with a smile of compassion, stating that I must be Kris. I had seen many of those smiles in the days of my own care.

I shivered at the sight, which I slowly held to my heart when she smiled. Frail and ghostly white and gray, my mother's spirit was hovering above us, watching.

"Well, what have you gone and done now, Mom?" I went for the jest in hopes that it would disguise my pain.

Johnny sat quietly to the side, respectfully.

Norma's crackly voice brought forth tears of pain and joy. "I am so glad to see you. I love you, Kris." My throat squeezed shut. My palms were sweating and my eyes dripped tears down my jacket, "Me too, Mom, me too."

Colon cancer had invaded her body over the last four or five years, according to the doctors. The invasion had progressed to Stage 4, which amounted to enough destruction of her body that the incision they'd made could not be closed. Norma weighed roughly one hundred and five this day in late June.

Over the next couple of days, we tried to convince Johnny to allow Norma to come home to Indiana. Johnny, always paranoid, a leftover from his days in the military, refused, leaving J. P. no other option than to accept rather than fight. Arrangements to comfort Norma in the poor shack they called home tore J. P. apart, and distanced him even more from his daughter. It was no longer a question of whether death was at hand; it was a matter of when it would show itself at Norma's door.

In the obnoxiously obtuse manner I had perpetuated, I decided that Norma would be fine, that the problem lay with the treatment, not the disease. I certainly had been told about the severity of Norma's illness, but I was good at denial, and truly had no idea of the consequences.

It seemed like forever before I returned to Indiana and the shell of my family there. In the same way my father before me had done, I let my emotions run cold and evaporate from view. As sober and stale as I had ever been, I felt a deep understanding of hopeless desperation.

Without rhyme, reason, or connection to the world around me, I used the next few weeks to drown even deeper into the abyss. Each day dragged into the next as I waited for the next phone call. Waking on the floor or sitting in the car I would realize I had failed to pick up my family at a prescheduled time or location, the errand boy on whom nobody could depend. Endless scrapes with the law continued. My insecurities were gaining strength as the fear set in deeper. I hid money and bottles of booze everywhere I could think of to be sure there would never come a time I would not have access to the one thing I required.

Finally, it came. Don's stern voice on the other end of the phone. "Kris, it's time for you to go."

This time it was a breezy fall afternoon when I left for the airport. Moist leaves skirted across the yard. My task was to arrive at death's door. I beckoned what sanity I could to present the reasonable facsimile of a normal man. The taxi ride from the airport in Arkansas was surreal and quiet. I almost asked the cab driver to drive right on past our destination, afraid of what I would see when I entered my mother's room. A room closely watched, I was certain, by the Devil and God alike.

Chapter 17

SUNDOWN

The medical center had that same smell and ominous lighting that makes the skin take on an unearthly shade of pale pink never seen anywhere else. Meeting me at the entrance was the loving figure of the man upon whom so many had depended, J. P.

"Hello, son, how was your trip down?" he asked, more as a formality than with an interest in the answer. At the touch of our hands, the tears spilled over and we held strong to the feeling of warmth the live hands offered. Our family had always touched, it seemed. Perhaps it was the only thread of likeness we shared. Minus the fingers to grasp, I still had the comfort of knowing this man cared for my life almost as much as did the woman I was here to see. But I did not want to see the truth.

We walked into the lobby and immediately Johnny and a nurse engulfed me. It was as if I were being briefed on a classified military assignment.

"Kris, what you're going to see is going to be hard," said the drill instructor. Never before had I witnessed the man so reduced. "Your mother doesn't look like herself anymore; she's lost a lot of weight. She hasn't eaten any food for several days."

Withering inside with each word, I internally begged him to stop his description. I replied, "Well, I can help with that part. I can get her to eat something, right?" Speaking as the jester, I played dumb to shift the subject of a conversation I knew nothing about.

The tone of the conversation remained somber, though, as the nurse continued to tell me about the equipment. I know they had coached her not to alarm me with details.

Reaching into my shallow soul, I limped into Norma's room. My Grandpa sat by the bed. The action slowed to a frame-by-frame exposure as I looked at the bed. The blankets rested on a silhouette of bones, sharp toes extending under the bed tray posted at the end. Her legs looked like the broken branches of a tree. I was startled and confused. Whose legs were they, whose feet? The skin had collapsed, shrink-wrapped over a collection of splinters with yellow nails at the end.

There was more space than body under the rest of the blanket. The fragile empty breathing corpse I identified as my forty-four-year-old mother. Her breasts and chest wheezed with each forcible push against the reaper's tug. The beauty of her green eyes was shadowed and secluded inside a face which no longer gleamed with jaded brilliance. The smile her mouth etched when she managed to pull her eyelids upwards disclosed a tarnished bar of ivory that had hushed an auditorium and crushed more than one man's purpose. Hair that stuck out from a misshapen dome of flesh curled around listlessly and fell to a pillow littered by other strands of her identity.

"Oh, honey," she said, and her body suddenly jerked violently, raging to escape. Her own recognition of her appearance was reflected in my eyes.

What I saw scared me so much that I didn't know what to do. Johnny and the nurse quickly settled her skeleton back to a resting place so she might gather her next breath. The drool easing from her lips was of a stench and color that only appears at death's entry. We sat to rest.

As I sat next to her and asked her questions of normal conversation, my powerlessness to grasp the seriousness of the situation was obvious. I insisted to myself that when her body regained strength we could fight this! That was, after all, the very message she had instilled in me, as I grew up so riddled with "challenges." "Fight, Kris, fight," was her motto to every potential defeat we might meet with my legs, feet, arms, or hands. Surely, fighting was appropriate here, too.

Surely she could fight just a little more.

I went out to the waiting room and cried for what felt like hours. Her once strong beauty-queen appearance was gone and what air could enter was quickly respirated, taking an ounce of life with it. Norma's life was ending, and soon. I was as a child—and that is actually what I was still— nothing but a child who had no idea of what it took to face death in its entirety as those around me had done so many times before. J. P. was about to lose the last of three women in his life in as little as two years. Not only was the core of our family now gone, so was the energy to support those of us left. The backbone of moral fiber that was my grandfather had been broken many times over, and I, fool that I was, had had no respect for his pain.

Even Johnny, in his selfishness, attempted to rouse himself to give homage to what would soon be Norma's memory, and had preformed a miracle of healing and comfort in her final days. It was all I could do to pull myself together enough to share what I knew were my last few moments with the angel who was about to leave me alone. Alone to face a war of terror, strife, and discouragement. I wanted to go with her on this last journey into death.

A day or two went by, hours filled with little talks, quiet window-watching, wiping drool, being excused from the room for the periodic nurse's duties. Duties this matriarch had once preformed for me.

During the next seventy-two hours, Mom took in some nutrition and her energy improved. She had refused treatment because of the advanced stage of the disease, but she was still sharp as a tack. I knew it wouldn't last, but I couldn't help the surge of hope it gave me. The storm was fast approaching.

We attempted short card games and found ourselves laughing about the past, our travels and mishaps now sources of pleasure. Song, dance, and food on an autumn day in Brown County allowed us to look away from the cracking skin around her mouth from lack of sustenance in the last weeks.

The days of love and of sharing, and of Aunt Charlotte's green bean casserole brought seductive memories of goodwill and sibling rivalry.

Memories of the escapades of a rambunctious boy who refused to pull cattails from the pond in the mid-summer heat and drove a truck in the middle of the desert. Recollections of times that in retrospect were carefree, times before I knew better. And memories of the precarious pleasures of a schoolgirl with her childhood sweetheart who now, in the face of life's eventual request, sat alongside the final destination.

Today, the clock on the wall spoke loudly, each click, each second. I slept huddled in the lounge, oblivious to the offers of comfort the attendants made. J. P. floated into the room and out, his expression more and more troubled with each pass. This time he stopped at my chair. "Maybe you should go in there now, Kris."

In my mind, my body sank to the floor, but I raised my head and sat up at attention. The very man who had taught me how to drink was sitting a few feet away and I found it ironic that what I really wanted to do was run in and do what we—I—had always done—grab a bottle and get started. Or maybe run to the truck and load up the fishing poles, yell at the dog, and drive away from our troubles. Instead, I prayed to God to please be with

215

me and protect my mother. I did not really believe He would do anything for me, but I did hope He would care for her, so I asked anyway.

The light in the room had been turned down to soften the bluish glare. With Johnny on the far side of the bed, I pulled up a chair next to her and gently rested my hands on hers. The one person who had taken comfort in holding my disfigured hands was now in need of my comfort and I didn't know what to say or do. I sat quietly, not trusting my voice, and watched.

After a few moments, Norma asked that the head of the bed be raised a bit. Johnny did as she requested, reaching over her frail torso and lifting her into a more elevated position. "There, how's that?" he asked.

I saw in his eyes the love of a young man for his sultry roller-skating girl of the past.

"Fine, just fine," she exhaled.

Norma turned to me then. I heard her words as if we were in a play, rehearsing our lines. "Kris, do you hold anything against me, son?"

Caught off guard by the question, I reacted without thinking. "No, Mom, of course not, I could never do that! I love you."

The next few moments are vacant to me, even to this day. But then, consoled by my answer, Norma asked for the bed to be lowered back down again.

As I watched, paralyzed into observance, Norma's eyes focused on the ceiling above and she began to vomit and convulse. Her face set in acceptance for the violence of the moment, she called on her will and slowly began to drown on the fluids she harbored. The milky green fluids that escaped her lips and pooled on the pillow repulsed my senses. Her chest pounded and thrashed as her heart seemed to explode with a wild and fierce fever. With each breath, her lungs inhaled more vomit, her heart beating in unison with each gasp. The noise was deafening. Death, Rapture Himself, was in this room.

Though the body had not yet succumbed, it was as though a stillness and peace began before the last pounding of her heart ceased and her hands, her bitterly cold hands, gave way to the surrender. All of her small skeleton shook and then, as abruptly as the seizure had begun, it subsided. Her hands stopped trembling. The sounds of slurping and expirating debris ceased. Silence came. Silence in the form of stillness; the strings that bound us together severed with a single swipe of the hand from God Almighty Himself.

Norma Jean's sun had set on the horizon forever.

* * *

Johnny reached across the bed and closed her eyes. The thought crossed my mind that perhaps he had done the same thing many times before in battle. Except this time, there was no victory or defeat. Only a moment recorded in time of another soldier who had served: Norma Jean.

I ran, hobbling and limping as cripples do. For that is what I was, a crippled freak who wanted to die! *KILL ME, DAMN IT, TAKE ME!*

I escaped to a corner in a room at the end of a hallway. I wept uncontrollably with a pain greater than any surgical procedure or cutting of bone fragments, a pain that cut deeper than any surgeon's knife could reach.

"Leave me alone, goddamnit, just fucking leave me alone!" I screamed at the shadowy image I felt standing behind me. The one person with whom I had a common bond, my grandfather, I now dishonored; his pain and loss at that moment had no meaning. He did not shirk from his responsibility to deliver me home to Indiana that night, however, and in complete isolation, we made the trip.

The experience changed my life; changed me. I would never be the same, nor would I recognize the fact that I was not able to deal with the crushing spiritual effects it would wield. Had I been better educated or perhaps if I had more of a connection with a religious faith, things would have been different. But I had neither and I became a casualty of circumstances once again. Disconnected from any purpose or direction, without values, the stage was set for my permanent demise.

Chapter 18

THREE HUNDRED SIXTY-FIVE DAYS

They say a loved one's life is reflected in the memories others express. I've also heard that if there is a trait you admire in someone who has passed, it is a sign of appreciation to make it your own. If this is true, then the Jim Beam I poured into my life was that. After all, Mom had drunk it with style and class.

My recall of events during that time is smudged at best, but at some point I remember waking from a drunken stupor on the living room floor. I had been awakened by Gail and her family who were taking out a collection of furniture and belongings. Empty bottles were scattered across the floor.

I made one demand only, "Don't take my whiskey!"

It mattered not that my daughter was leaving or my wife, who had been loyal and steadfast. She was leaving to protect what sanity she had left. I had become a thief who had stolen every ounce of dignity she had as well. Thank God she left; it was the only thing she could do. Her seat in heaven had been reserved a long time before, I knew that. It would be years before I saw the child again.

* * *

I was broke. I couldn't pay the rent or the electric bill and it was cold outside. My leg was beginning to show signs of failure, what with the lack of food and care I was providing my body. So I did what every other Carter had done before me: I looked to Flossie. Surely, her overwhelming aspiration to protect and nurture her family would protect me in these times. I begged my way into her guestroom, into safety. But I was so void of the ability to show gratitude that I used any excuse I could to discourage her love and to exit the safety of her arms. After only last a few days, my blundering mania took me away towards the life I had left in Logansport before my mother's death.

As parallel lives go, there were many passersby. A young boy in Kokomo had drawn the attention of the entire world with his contraction of a new disease they called AIDS. His name, Ryan White, was everywhere, including on the television that played behind the smoke-filled bar where I found myself one day. Elton John dedicated his song *Goodbye Norma Jean* to this little boy.

I drifted in and out of flophouses that year, occasionally staying with a woman who could tolerate me for a day. I would like to say that my actions were due to a pathetic loneliness, expressed in self-pity, loathing, and sadness. In reality, I remember nothing of the way I felt, none of the people I met, and none of the places I stayed.

When I sobered up long enough to have a hangover, my only thought was for finding the next pool table or an ear to bend. Personal hygiene took a distant second place to chasing the oblivion I wanted. It was silence I so hoped to secure, every chance I could. Whether it was a bottle of rum or the next new drug in town, I was willing to risk any moral or physical price to achieve it.

When once upon a time I had been received as an unfortunate misfit, now I was nothing more than another misplaced vagabond, no longer welcome. By now the summer's warm campfires and quiet backyards were no longer offering the shelter I needed. I knew of only one home that would allow me to cross the threshold. All other bridges and trails had long since been swept away, crumbled under the weight of distrust, false truths, and immoral actions.

As I drove the broken-down, stolen, drunk-mobile across a canvas of fall-colored roads to Flossie's house, I noticed nothing, heard nothing, and prayed that nothing would soon arrive. Thoughts of how death would arrive were my only company.

Each hour was heavier than the one before. When I arose on this day, I had felt an inkling of determination to do something, anything that would take me outside myself. The young boy from Kokomo had passed away. Lucky him. His funeral was an open invitation to the entire state of Indiana and I decided I too would attend in honor of my mother. Did she not deserve that kind of celebration as well?

"Where are you going, all fancied up there?" asked Flossie.

"I'm going to a funeral in Indianapolis, Ryan's. It starts at 2:00. I'm going to be late."

I continued with my effort, knowing all along in my soul that I would never make the trudge into the cathedral for fear of embarrassment. As I drove the one-hour journey, I must have listened to *Candle in the Wind* eight or nine times.

Goodbye Norma Jean (I never understood when or how to say goodbye)
Though I never knew you at all (I had never matured enough, nor cared to)
You had the grace to hold yourself (above all others)
While those around you crawled (we scurried like rats)
Crawled out of the woodwork (every turn and opportunity)
And they whispered into your brain (seduced into lives beyond understanding)
They set you on a treadmill (from one side of the country to the next)
And they made you change your name (my family name was gone)

And it seems to me you lived your life (apart, and never a chance to share)

Like a candle in the wind (tattered, scuffed from the roads traveled)

Never knowing who to cling to (Johnny, J. P., Don, Flossie, me...)

When the rain set in (sadness from another failed attempt at life's awards)

And I would've like to have known you (more than anything in the world)

But I was just a kid (twenty-three years old when you left)

Your candle burned-out long before (the flame stifled by time)

Your legend ever did (this too shall pass...)

Loneliness was tough (every chance I prayed for your heart to be filled)

The toughest role you ever played (a battle for social acceptance)

Hollywood created a superstar (your beauty, grace, and allure)

And pain was the price you paid (solitude, nights of regret)

Even when you died (never accepted or obeyed)

Oh, the press still hounded you (the writings distorted to this day)

All the papers had to say (the blame and guilt of a broken heart)

Was that Marilyn was found in the nude (naked from the eyes of truth)

Goodbye Norma Jean (dear God in heaven, why her; why now?)

Though I never knew you at all (I want to know more, give me a chance)

225

You had the grace to hold yourself (grace was all that I knew of her...)

While those around you crawled (no one was worthy of her)

Goodbye Norma Jean (see ya, Mom, I love you so much)

From the young man in the 22nd row (always watching from afar)

Who sees you as something more than sexual (the matriarch)

More than just our Marilyn Monroe (more than a wife or mother)

Your candle burned-out long before (your frail body is gone)

Your legend ever did (your soul lives on with me today...)

As I sat in the parking lot of that church, the limos arrived, bringing noted celebrities like Elton John, Michael Jackson, and others, and I wondered if they knew of the lives they so randomly touched.

If there really is a power or an energy of good out there, I thought, then why is it such a reach to think we could connect with it? If we really do have auras, those life forces some profess to see, then on that day I witnessed mine as it sunk beneath the realm of hopelessness into the purest despair. The end was near and my ability to express sorrow for another could not be summoned from the pile of rubbish that was my own personal landfill. Weeping, shaking violently from the lack of alcohol and cocaine, I removed myself from the church parking lot just as I had arrived, transparently. Perhaps later that day the internal man I was would match the suit I wore, but the odds favored a more typical harbor of worship for drunks like me.

I do have vague recollections of pathetic attempts to beg another dollar from Flossie from the vantage point of the floor. My efforts met with a firm resistance, the kind you would expect from a matriarch of this caliber. Flossie had the values of a prior generation and ilk and boozing away money was the Devil's work. Liquor had caused nothing but heartache and another offspring to support, and clearly she had had enough. Her apple-pie welcome had worn off long ago and the pot of beans was beginning to burn.

The day took on an odor like none before. My misery and soul sickness was fluid, pouring out of me at every turn, in every bar, at every pool table. I never wanted to see the sunrise again. I had not thought it possible to reach another point of no return—how could there be so many?

I was drinking and taking as many drugs as I could find, but it appeared that my state of mind remained the same. Oblivion would not come. I could no longer imagine my life with or with out my addictions, but it was as if I were immune to the concoctions with which I fed my body.

As the sun fell to its final resting place outside the window of the tavern where I sat, my idea of leaving involved not only the building, but the ground on which it resided. The method had come to me in a brief moment of intellect as the bartender served my poison. Tonight I would leave as the coward I had become, in a blaze of glory.

Finally, my life would account for something. Sorrow would fill the halls and thoughts of those who knew of my existence and they would challenge their own values and judgments.

My God, how sunken I had become.

Knocking quietly on the door of a comrade, I drank, hoping this would be my last stop. Intervention by a divine power which I had no believable evidence existed was the only alternative.

Not to worry, though, there was no response and I lived on.

As I walked away, I wept again, as I had so much these last few weeks. It was almost a year to the day of Norma's passing and I suspected my tolerance for the memories which were sure to come would not bear the pain.

I lay back in the seat of the small two-door Mazda that barely had space for one person. Looking up through the hole in the roof I wondered what it would have been like had I never burdened the planet with my birth. Might Norma have lived the storybook life she deserved? Would my daughter Vera be a happier person without the shame of my antics to keep her company in her old age? Without the Carter family's misdeeds, would Flossie have a life of grace and security? I couldn't make sense of it—any of it. I screamed, I whispered, I spoke to God as if He were above me, in person.

"What, God? What is it? Can you save me?

"God help me; if you're there and you care for a soul like me, show yourself now!

"Give me proof!" I demanded.

I waited but nothing came.

"If you don't prove yourself to me now, that's it. I've had enough. I'm checking out!" I recognized my own demands for what they were—those of a spoiled, egocentric child of his parents at Christmas.

I pulled out onto the local highway. I knew the road, the trees, the telephone poles, and ditches available to shelter the evidence. I took my empty shell and aligned the speeding mass of steel and glass to carry out my selfish, self-centered needs.

Silence and lack of pain was all I really ever wanted. As the speedometer rose above 90 MPH, I watched things unfold in slow motion. I took my right hand and placed it in my lap. I positioned the sole able finger of my left hand inside the steering wheel with a flip of the wrist. I closed my eyes, rested my head back, and waited for the silence to begin

as I felt the car begin to shift sideways. The tires started to screech and my

body leaned with the pull.

I recall nothing beyond this point. I heard nothing. The absence of pain

and access to death coupled with silence had finally arrived.

See, there is no God.

* * *

Time was empty; it paused unwittingly.

My suicide attempt left me with the car crushed around my less-than-

five-foot body. I was on top of the drive shaft and between the bucket

seats. The cartilage in my chest and back had been shredded and torn. My

face was studded with broken glass and blood was everywhere. My legs

were battered and bruised, flakes of severed glass particles protruding

from their flesh. My hands shook in terror. I hung in an upside-down,

crooked position, which led me to think I was in a ditch. Was this the feeling I had missed so many years ago when Hollywood had lost his life on a similar stretch of road? "God, help me!" I cried.

The officer hovered over me. He assumed my tire had gotten stuck in the gravel and I had overcorrected. I let him believe it. I replied with a strained "yes," and that was the end of the discussion.

I can say with out reservation that as the car slid and tumbled over the pavement, as it went crashing and splintering into the night, nothing could have saved me but the divine hand of God, which had reached itself into that battered car and wrapped its palm around me to comfort and protect me.

I had raged and revolted against the force of creation responsible for my grotesque image for all the years of my life, but in that moment I had experienced the touch of God's hand. I suddenly knew that His life force existed; I had no question, no doubt. It would be many years before I again felt His touch as I had that day. But my belief and trust in a God who knows me, who resides over our souls, who shares His bounty of love, has never wavered again.

It would also be years before I could accept this divine love. Nevertheless, I cannot tell you that the experience did not happen, nor that the seconds inside that air-bound coffin have not changed my life. I became unequivocally convinced in the established the presence of God.

The hushed whisper was replete with more parental love than I had ever imagined could be. "It's okay. I've got you now, I've got you now!"

Then the long silent pause, disguised as a spiritual experience.

* * *

It is said that to show contempt before investigation is a sign only of ignorance. If that holds weight, then it was up to me to investigate how to fill my soul, clean up my life, and make my heart safe. Where would the power come from that would enable me to live a purposeful life, a journey without gluttony and sloth? Was there really a place where my life, my deformed and misshapen existence, could serve as a light of reason and complete its circle? After all, so far this life had not been a welcoming place of comfort. For some reason, though, I found myself hovering somewhere above the plane where I once walked, having been given another chance. Was this an illusion, a Midway escape that would only later reveal a dusty trick, a bit of glitter or a shell game played to swindle?

I would like to say the tale ends here, with the breath of life, with the gift I had been given. Perhaps you already feel you know the conclusion. If that's the case, I beg your indulgence.

Chapter 19

LIVING ONE DAY

I had been delivered to the county jail after a brief exam at the local hospital; my weakened body now lay resting on the cold floor. Out of pity, perhaps, the jailer was kind enough to provide me a thin mattress to aide my braced back and shoulders. I shivered for the next four or five hours until an escort came to take me to the courthouse, where I would be issued my next punishment. With that observation, I was afraid that nothing had really changed.

I wore the favorite color for fools, an orange jumpsuit, which barely cloaked my bloody shirt, evidence of the night before. The parade of captured entered the room and justice was dished out for each sorry soul. My turn came next.

From the bench above, a woman in robes bellowed, "Mr. Carter, what is it that you feel we should do in this case?"

She was asking me, the jester?

She shook her head. "There really is nothing this court can do to punish you beyond your own self-imposed pain."

I was witnessing an act of forgiveness, but I did not understand.

I quivered out a response, "I am not sure, Your Honor. I need help."

"Yes, yes, you do, sir. I will order you released on your own recognizance. The officer will escort you to the bus terminal." She pointed to a man of average stature who resembled a certain Marine I had known. "You will have the fare to travel to the hospital. If you fail to go, Mr. Carter, I will not be this forgiving again."

I knew the grace of His hand was touching my shoulder. As I walked along next to this man in a crisp uniform, I felt both humbled and humiliated, aware of the eyes riveted to my tattered body as I boarded the city bus. The driver told me to sit behind him.

My arrival at the Middletown Center was short and blurred with introductions and papers. "I don't want to hear shit about God," I sputtered, cocksure fool that I was. "Just get me off the booze and drugs." My rebellious approach had little resolve at its core, which I'm sure was clear to everyone around me.

In the days that followed, I suffered the typical DTs and raging heaves that dried my lips to a crackling, bloody mess. The sweat and fevers were offset only by the showers, offered twice daily.

Before the week was up, I was eating a "light diet" food tray with others in the cafeteria, people whom I would not know outside a tavern or drug house. But was I not one of them? I was more concerned that I would be recognized and that it would embarrass my family.

At the treatment facility, we were soon cornered off into either "Buzz-heads" or "Rednecks." I took great pride in being a Buzz-head. Meetings and activities were scheduled much of the day. This was a thirty-day inpatient service and I was still not sure how I'd come to be there because I had no way to pay for it. I later discovered my label of "hopeless," or "indigent."

During the second week we were to attend an AA meeting downstairs. In my mind I pictured a room full of shriveled dried-out old men. Truthfully, I saw no need to go. I was not one of *them*. But when I got there, I saw I'd been mistaken about what an alcoholic looked like, how an alcoholic behaved. In this room sat clean, well-dressed, and well-spoken men and women.

Although I looked briefly at the men, the women caught my attention. Not because of sexual attraction or lust, but because I just did not believe that women of this quality could have come from the same gates of hell that I had. Maybe this twelve-step way of life had merit after all. Perhaps, for once in a long while, I should shut up and listen.

The fact is that I listened about as much as I talked. I talked a lot! It seemed I had an answer for every question and a question for every puzzle. I had lived in a fantasy world of my own creation for so long that I had developed a hard shell of isolation. I had worked hard to separate myself from those who I feared would get close enough to peer over the wall and discover there was nothing but an empty shell.

The shell was cracking open.

On the twenty-eighth day of treatment, after many days of individual talks with my counselor, he directed me to leave. "Kris, there's nothing else we can do for you here." Pete was always very direct. "You're either going to die drunk or recover in AA. You need to go."

The chill I felt was frightening. After the isolation of birth, life, alcoholism, and a failed suicide…now I had failed to be good enough to save? Where was the God who reached in and saved? Was there no grace to be found?

Storming out of Pete's office, I crashed out of the treatment center onto the street in front of the hospital, looking desperately to find the closest bar or tavern. I was driven to finish what I had started twenty-eight days earlier. My goal at this moment was to buy the largest bottle of rum I could find and join it with any other spirit available, anything that could take my soul and burn it with fury!

Somehow, I do not know why or how, the only answer that came was silence.

I found myself in a parallel space where grace once again gave me a chance.

It was another miracle. I do not know what I did, where I went, with whom I spoke. Somehow my flesh was transported to a place of rest. I found myself at the High Street Methodist Church at 8:00 p.m., not knowing the content of the last nine hours. Once more I had only the grace of God to account for that time. His hands brushed away all worldly understanding of my actions and efforts. The gift of sobriety had remained, and so had His hand of glory in my life.

* * *

Once again my grandmother opened her arms to me and I lived in her home for the next couple of years. It was relatively easy, although I'm sure it served for good gossip among the other remaining family members. Flossie never made me feel I was a burden. In fact, well into her eighties now, she often commented on how glad she was that I was there. I know her love for me was true, and I wished I might have been a better grandson. We ate many dinners together, after which we spent an hour or two watching television. Her social life was still full of church activities, and there were many days we did no more than pass each other in our travels.

It was while I was being exposed to a method of dealing with life without the aide of booze or drugs that I met a man named Bob. Bob attended the same meetings as I did and lived only a few short blocks from us. For about six months I could be seen waiting and listening for the honk of the horn of Bob's old red truck to take us to our next meeting. One day I learned that Bob had cancer; his weak body had developed a tumor behind his esophagus and he was slowly choking to death. I was shattered.

The days slipped quickly away as Bob weakened. One day, a friend came to visit Bob while he was resting at his mother's home.

Ben reached down to Bob, whose voice rattled and chattered for air. "Can I do anything for you? Get you anything?" he asked gently.

Bob's eyes took on a mischievous look. He took another breath and said, "Yeah, stay sober."

I watched as this man showed me that I could not only live my life with dignity and integrity, but that I could also die with dignity. I had never believed that a person such as I could have that privilege. Until that moment, even sober, I had been convinced my life was not worthy of a dignified existence. Bob died on the anniversary of my ninth month of sobriety, and I was still sober by the grace of God and the fellowship of His children.

I walked to meetings on a regular basis since I had not the money or the legal ability to drive again. The snow at this time of year was thick, but the walking seemed to strengthen my body—other than my right leg, which was always in pain. My body had suffered years of neglect by this time and had never served much of a value in terms of long-term stability. I had never been able to feel anything from the knee down and with the chill of winter I had started to take evening baths to warm the dead flesh. I lost my misshapen toenails regularly during the cold months, just one of my ongoing struggles.

I had found a safe harbor for a while, but I could see that the time was growing closer when I would have to survive on my own again. Although I had yet to establish a livelihood, I was eager to try. My driver's license reestablished, I asked if Don would help me purchase a car. He was hesitant, and I couldn't blame him; he'd been witness to my misguided life for a long time. They say it takes a village to raise a child. In my life, the village was made up of a few good people. I had never been alone in my efforts, and I was finally beginning to see that.

I began to return to my artistic endeavors, including doing small items for storefront decorations. In one such case, I entered a contest for a local grocery display. The theme was the space shuttle program. The project was grand in its scale and technical detail. The lights, motion, and colors were sure to win the national contest that was coming up at the end of the week. What we didn't know was that the Challenger disaster was about to occur.

We still experienced a bit of notoriety, but to a much more somber degree, reflecting the emotions associated with the tragedy. I questioned my ability to ever rise above the status of a failure, but I had committed to a life of optimism and held on.

Truth be told, my emotional maturity at the age of twenty-eight was no more than that of a ten-year-old. My social and emotional skills were certainly stuck at that time, when I'd started to drink and quarantine myself from everyone around me. They say that our lives can never grow past our fear. If that is true, God help me, for I am afraid of everything for I understand nothing. I had never developed the potential to roll with the punches or take things with a grain of salt. My emotional well had been dry for a very, very long time. And now it seemed that every time I trusted, loved, or attempted to share myself, I failed or they died! Of true friendship

I knew not! I knew only of leaving and of being left, and that nothing ever lasts.

The bottom line was that I was lonely. I found myself wanting for the pleasures of a woman and knew my respect for my grandmother would not allow this to happen. I needed to find a place of my own again.

Advising me as always, her feathers proudly displayed in a stance of protection, Flossie said, "You sure about this, Kris? Why don't you just stay here and save a little money."

"No, no, I think I can do it this time, Grandma. I can get a good job somewhere and now that I have a car again, I'll be fine." I sounded afraid even to my own ears.

Later that spring, I made a stab at becoming an entrepreneur. I was under the impression that the local area needed a singles club. All you had to do was have a meeting, right? People show up, you take a few names, and have a party! I convinced a pal to join my expedition and we went forward.

I had not been at the first meeting more than a few minutes when I was struck dumb by a vision in pink slacks, a snug sweater, blond curls, and a full set of red lips. It occurred to me that this was the reason for all my efforts at becoming a more well-balanced person.

I was in lust!

Chapter 20

THE CHASE

The chase to become a man and a solid fixture of society became my sole objective. Always wanting to fit in, I decided that I would finish the schooling I had begun years before. I still had the same deformities and temperament, but this time I approached my education with purpose and entered a twenty-four-month engineering program. I developed a taste and knack for things of precision, including automation and robotics. The computer-aided design systems of the world had just begun to evolve into user-defined tools that allowed people like me to learn.

"Learn well and quickly" became my motto. I finished my degree in fewer than thirteen months, taking twenty-two credit hours each quarter, with a GPA of 3.89. An instructor who had so kindly taken a few moments of instruction to show me some fundamental skills also arranged for a job interview prior to graduation, and I secured it on the spot. For the first time I became accepted because of my capacities. It was nine months later and I needed to earn a wage that would allow me to support my newly born son, a result of the encounter with the vision in pink with the full red lips, and my daughter who was now several years old. Perhaps this square peg had found a home?

* * *

Soon the chase had led me to secure another position as a subcontractor. I had grown to see myself as a kind of professional hired gun. I found that this form of work provided me the means to focus on my talent to perform in a world few understood, all the while keeping a distance from disclosing my failings. Troubleshooting provided the perfect solution.

Soon I was developing software solutions for the manufacturing industry or clients who needed to perform complex mathematical equations for automated machinery. Communications around engineering platforms or specialized product configurations for the automotive industry provided a foundation for me in a world where the language was understood by very few. In this world I easily increased my worldly value and provided economic security for my children. Unfortunately, the trail I had once followed made the life of this divorced father painfully expensive.

After a couple of years of doing the next right thing and feeling the strength of a new personal identity, I began to realize that I did not feel the satisfaction I craved...that something was missing. I knew it was the all but completely absent connection with my children. Long, emotionally driven squabbles between two distant people were recreating a void inside me equal to that which I had owned once before. I slept restlessly at night and discovered a yearning to feed that perverted soul sickness again.

I began to feed my loneliness with sexual meetings, chance encounters with women I met at the local pool hall or lounge. Drinking tonic water and having a pocket full of money to flash around secured a night's sexual entertainment, often with only a smile. It seemed money had a way of balancing flaws otherwise too numerous ignore.

I hid my physical deformities with miscellaneous clothing and dimly lit rooms, feeling as I did when I hid behind my art. I used a cigarette as a prop. Holding the tobacco stick above my lips, it offered a screen of smoke and the need for a hand gesture, which obstructed the view from those who dared to look. Nothing kept the questions at bay, however. "What happened to you?"

It did not take long for this downward trend to mount into a pile of debris that I could no longer drag behind me. My son had already been removed from the area, taken against all rules of decency, and the agony of my loneliness catapulted into a form that resembled emotional suicide. My work had flourished, but now met with resistance due to my current level of distraction.

I found my car driving aimlessly across vast areas of land. It was another Indiana autumn. I would have preferred to eliminate myself, but the God in whom I still believed reassured me that He would not leave me to wail alone in misery. I went back to the only place I knew where I could rescue the collection of scars I had become. I admitted myself into a psychiatric facility to release the need to die.

When I heard the sound of the electronic door slam behind me, I found myself stone sober and with a heart that ached with a grief I had never dealt with before. I had no choice but to open my soul, to bleed in tears of hope and perhaps find freedom from this burden, a burden rooted in the belief that appearance, rather than quality, made the person. Ironic as it might be, I discovered that I had judged all my life as people had judged me—on physical appearance. I had gauged the mistakes of nature as a way or measuring worth as a human being. The square peg had burrowed a home so deep within my mind that only the equestrians of doom could provide an exit from the despair.

The path to sanity called but the right steps were still vague. My professional life was in conflict with my need to find my son. In the end, never having a true understanding of financial responsibility, I followed my heart to Ohio, where he was with his mother. I had to place my son above all else or I would always ask myself why I had not. I left after a birthday party for the woman I was dating at the time, a woman with love as genuine as her lovely red hair. Since then I tried to find this woman on many occasions, but I never saw her again.

When I arrived in the town where my son Shane and his mother lived, I rented an apartment to secure a safe place to visit. The anger over money had drawn a tone of resentment that I soon would use as a weapon against my lusting error. The daily challenges to see Shane or become a part of his life met with resistance. On many occasions, I found no one home to witness my attempts to visit.

It didn't take long before my funds began to disappear. I needed to find a job in the area to support my obsession to be near him, but the only thing I saw in the paper was driving a tractor-trailer in Dayton. Though by now my legs had started to weaken, as predicted, and the constant use of my hands caused them to ache from progressive osteoarthritis, I again saw no choice. I needed the money.

I took a Greyhound to Dayton and enrolled in the driving school. Again, I underestimated both the confidence and knowledge I would need, and found myself in a position where I felt out of my element. Learning to gauge distance, to handle the massive foot pedals, and to steer a full-size wheel that had no sympathy for my arms or fingers, was nearly impossible. After six weeks, failure was again in sight.

Where was I to go? What was I to do? I had no home other than a fleabag motel and a car that had seen better days. When I heard from Flossie that she needed help, I went home.

* * *

Flossie's compassion, love, and patience summoned yet another much-needed dose of energy. I had not thought that courage was what I needed, but now I realized that's exactly what it would take to face the powerful force of indifference and strife I encountered. Flossie once again rescued my heart with her generosity, but I would never stop feeling guilt over everything she had given me. Honestly, I felt it was God's turn to care for me again.

I always thought I had gift to call on His strength when I needed it. But like the footprints in the sand, I knew no understanding. It would be many years before I would know how He had carried me, before I would allow His work in my life to reflect an image upon which others could draw. Even now, I question the relativity of what exists in a parallel space now and of the One who walks with us in times of trouble. And even in my worst times, I have always retained a need to understand how the touch of Divine Guidance, so often misconstrued by intellect or emotional foolishness, really works. Would He who knew reveal such a fatal secret? I am afraid such knowledge will always remain hidden.

My nights were filled with religious study, broken sleep, and coffee, and spiritual pursuits became my path to wisdom. I engulfed myself into every drop of literature I could find, the writings of Catholics, Methodists and others, such as the Oxford Group. My studies filled my mind with visions of release from the hell I knew on Earth. The message seemed to be that for most of us, the price of admittance to freedom of spirit came by way of the rail of misfortune. I witnessed miracles as I partook of and accepted the praise from experiences which gasped at the Glory each and every time. I had once been told by a man of character that if I placed my life on a spiritual foundation my life's remaining struggles would be cast aside. It brought to mind the snippet of wisdom, the vision of right and wrong, that Norma had imparted night after night as I suffered with physical pain: "This too shall pass."

I spent many a night like this, secluded inside a small apartment, a short stroll away from the library, my utility bills reflecting that of an early-to-bed, early-to-rise approach to each day. Drawing small funds from my unemployment checks (for which I was eligible after the last "great stab") my needs at the most fundamental level were filled. My need for intellectual stimulation was supplied by Scripture and history, and in its acquisition I experienced a flash of lightning in the form of a quiet spiritual awakening. I soon learned, however, that spiritual awakening would not be enough to deflect the challenges of the practicalities of daily living.

C h a p t e r   2 1

THERE SHE IS

Once bitten, twice shy should have been my theme song for the duration

of my life. My love for the scent of a woman and need for her touch,

however, kept me searching for connection. And when I opened the door of

the singles club that night, there she was. She stood in the corner, her stature

equal to mine. The glow around her face told me she would be important to

me.

"Would you like to dance?" I asked, expecting rejection.

There was a pause and the usual sweep of the eyes over my appearance.

But, as she lowered her drink to the table behind her, she turned back and

said, "Sure, come on, I'll dance with you."

I'm sure she noticed that my capacity to dance was not what one would

expect from two functioning legs and arms of equal length. Perhaps she

granted me a dance to view the entertainment. I had not changed the style of my attire and have to admit to having the loud dress of the jester I had tried so hard to promote in the past. I noted that this woman's motions were as sporadic as mine, however, and that she periodically sent a glance and a smile in my direction to make sure we avoided any mishaps.

The song ended, and I felt as timid as a mouse. When she grabbed my hand in acceptance as we made our way back to the table, I was amazed. Perhaps for most, a simple brush of the hand is nothing more, but for those of us who hide ourselves to prevent curiosity, I knew this meant a host of questions would soon follow.

"Thank you for the dance," I said formally, "it was my pleasure. Perhaps we can do it again later?" I held my breath as I waited for her rejection.

"Sure. Just ask me later," she said, adding, "my name is Patty."

What was I supposed to do now? I had just met a woman who was direct, strong, and graceful. I knew I would not be able to stay away.

I bided my time and then, calling on some false courage from my elixir of Seven-Up, I stood with the start of a slow song and began my approach.

SLAM. Her hand reached out to another as I walked towards her. I feigned a polite pass, but it felt like a slap in the face. I strolled past as if on my way to the rest room with improvised purpose. The look on her face told me there was a game on.

After watching jealously as she danced in the arms of another man, I became determined it would not get the better of me. I had not felt these queasy feelings of childhood playground antics for a long time. But I was pleased to think that just maybe there was a spiritual connection between us and that there was a possibility of something more.

I had spent twenty minutes in that gray-lit room deciphering and creating my entire future with a woman I had just met and danced with once.

I waited for my energy level to return and then spent the next two hours entangled in her arms, mind, and smile. When the evening ended I escorted her to her car and asked for her phone number. When she replied with a confident "yes," I kissed her good-bye as I had rehearsed for the last hour. The taste of her lips and heat that rushed across my skin left me intoxicated.

I waited impatiently for the socially acceptable seventy-two hours to pass before I placed the call. I asked her to join me for dinner. I was in love.

This was a woman with whom I felt I could live forever. A single mother, she was both kind and a lady. Her family reflected the kindness I remembered from my early childhood and the ideal lives in the bedtime stories Norma read to me. Even more exciting was the moment of loving reception of my deformed body.

Never had I revealed myself to any woman the way I could with this woman. Why? Because I felt accepted!

They say doubt is the Devil's tool. Certainly it has hounded my every step. A closet pessimist, I have waded through pain, agony, disappointment, and their consequences. I knew I was letting my adolescent feelings distort my perspective, but I also knew that doubt shadows the glory of the sun every chance it gets. I knew that as long as this woman joined in, I would explore this journey of life to the end.

* * *

I needed to renew my relationship with a professional life. Surely a life of poverty would not be appreciated by such a woman. I was still marketable, but it had been a year since I had touched a machine or a computer.

One day I met Patty by chance at a church meeting. As with all God's interventions, it was unexpected yet synchronistic when the minister spoke to the crowd and asked for "the person in the room who needs a job to speak up." Patty gave me a nudge and I stood up and introduced myself.

I told the room about my skills and needs and in a moment a man across the room stood to say perhaps he could introduce me to someone he knew. As I slowly sat back down into the pew, I felt the palm of His grace wrap His love around us both, and knew that my immediate future would be secure. Though we were not married, I was experiencing a union of the soul with the woman who sat next to me.

The man in the church was as good as his word and soon I was gainfully employed again, in a position that would provide the financial means for me to support a family, my family! We soon joined under one roof with the partial acceptance of Patty's daughter. Unfortunately, Patty's son had a difficult time understanding my need to be with his mother. I wish I could have changed that dynamic, but it was never to be.

C h a p t e r   2 2

FINANCIAL INSECURITY

Ca-ching! It worked: Place God first and material wealth follows. I did it correctly. I understood, I worked, and I was found worthy! I had the skill, I had the knowledge, I had the house, I had the real estate, I had the cars, I had the money, I had the Girl. Finally, I had the power to control my life!

With the skill-set I developed, I became nationally recognized as a leading developer in the CAD-CAM industry. I was making a fortune by writing languages nobody but a robot could understand. My talents allowed me to start naming my own price again, but this time it was different; it was the mid '90s and success was everywhere.

I began buying rental properties with tenants as difficult as bad stepchildren—and I should know! Calls in the middle of the night pushed my acceptance to the limit. I denied that I might be crossing over into the realm of greed and focused on keeping my feet firmly on the ground for the benefit of my family. Christmases got larger, vacations more luxurious, and the spending easier every day.

Companies across the country began asking for my services and so the need to travel mounted. I saw the pattern beginning to take shape once more. Again I chose to look away from the truth about my actions and the repercussions of those actions. I ventured out as a hired gun. The database of clients grew. So did the toll on my physical, emotional, and spiritual health.

Patty and I were living separate lives due to my traveling and her social environment of success and suburban entertaining. Our home won the Neighborhood Beautification Award and I constructed a huge deck to impress my family. By now, the children were much older and had moved out, although they visited daily. My efforts to gain a connection to my own children had not been particularly successful either. By now my daughter blamed me for her troubles and my son had become unreachable.

Another holiday season had gone by and it was a cold February. A customer in Indiana wanted an estimate and analysis of their operations. On completion of the evaluation, I had recommended a revamp of systems that would need a week's work. Even though my billing rates had begun to exceed thousands a week, this job would send my earnings over the top. I worked two hundred ten hours straight that week, rarely stopping to sleep.

About a hundred hours into the project, I received a call that shook my heart. J. P. had passed away the night before and his funeral was scheduled for the following day. Saddened and exhausted, I arranged for a driver to take me to Muncie for the service. I spent the five-hour trip there and back sleeping.

At the funeral, I found myself counting the number of faces I recalled from a childhood of fear. I had never felt wholly connected to the cast of characters, most of them strangers by now. I had loved in the only way I knew how, but too much of my own misery had been rolled into the mix. One thing was clear, though, in the pain etched on their faces as they said a last teary goodbye to the last member of the once strong tribe.

The cousins who once danced across the yard in Brown County wept at the memories. I saw a void in their midst which must have always been transparent. Each of them carried his and her own burden and chain of terror, and every thought of heightened indulgence from a family perceived to be normal escaped them as they walked away, a cold symbol of silence for another patriarch gone.

I heard about my Uncle Fred that day as well. It turns out my Uncle Fred, whom I had adored, had opened his home to a young man who needed some place to stay and help with transportation to a job. Fred's kindness was rewarded by this man with a pistol shot to Fred's head as he slept. The man then stole Fred's truck, the very one Fred had used to help his new friend. Sickened by the lack of honor which had been the demise of my uncle, I only managed to get through the rest of the funeral.

I felt solemn on the journey back. I had experienced an emotional breakdown and had reached inside with determination to achieve—in fact, surpass—the goals I set. But what was next?

I completed the job and collected the large sum for my work. The organization then offered me a position of permanent employment. It might have seemed like the perfect job, but my need to rest took precedence.

After a few days' rest, Patty and I took a trip to the Caribbean. Rejuvenated by the warmth and beauty, in a moment of enthusiasm, I married my best friend in a tropical garden.

It was not long after our return that I accepted the position that had been offered to me before we'd left on our trip. It came with a ridiculous amount of money to which I had never expected them to agree. We began our search for a new home on the lake. The realtor showed us a house with sixteen-foot cathedral ceilings, a cedar great room, a fireplace, formal dinning room, three bedrooms, Florida room, swimming pool, and one hundred twenty feet of prime waterfront. The house had some flaws, but our excitement overshadowed them. I had found the place I wished to die. Now, if I could only keep it afloat.

A year after moving to this heaven on earth, my position at the company became challenging due to personality conflicts with the comptroller. I drew on my contacts in Chicago and began traveling again. Patty was left alone in a new town without family support. If I could turn back the clock, it was here I would do it.

My journeys began to yield fewer funds to support our high-end lifestyle and my tries at gambling the balance started to show signs of collapse. After a family reunion to show off our extravagant home, I once again felt the pressure to disconnect. I was afraid of failure and therefore I began to fail.

My father, who had once reigned with wealth in Indianapolis, had lost his fortune and returned to Indiana a broken soul. His knock on my door excited me. To think that I could be of service to him! But true to his nature of emotional coolness, he rejected my offers.

Years later Patty found out that Don had found himself a small Tudor house only twenty minutes away. He was living alone, separated from the core of what life had given him. Money had only patched the holes left by his broken story and the icy relationships his spirit had created along the way. He had never called us, nor did he return our efforts to communicate.

* * *

I had built a house of cards and I shouldn't have been surprised when it began to crumble. Gambling to support short-term financial voids was no way to fill the gaps now revealing themselves. The ship had taken on more water than it would hold and the stress was adding to the toll on my body.

In the months previous, I had begun to experience my first heart problem and suffered extended discomfort and pain. By now, my right leg and hip no longer responded to the multiple Aleves I swallowed every day. Pepto-Bismol was now a staple of my diet. When asked, my reply was that I felt "a bit tender under the weather," but would be fine soon. All along I knew that damage from a budding ulcer was gaining headway. With the severe risk of colon and liver cancer, heart-related concerns, lack of mobility, and limb weakness, my body had become a battleground.

While working a job in Louisville, I met a doctor who offered me shots of Cortisone to relieve the immediate pain and allow me to walk without resultant stares or questions. I would survive, no matter the cost!

My character was quickly evaporating against the backdrop of fear. The religious training, the education, the spiritual awakening, and the deep need to interact with those around me was being replaced by a renewed need for isolation. I disappeared into dark rooms to sip a tonic water and to recapture precarious pleasures of the past and temporary relief through physical therapy, but the need to escape grew. Through massage, I found someone who would listen to my stories of pain. In turn, I received comfort.

In one such meeting, I found myself talking about my economic woes. I had scrambled over the past few days to secure a large sum of money from my contacts in Chicago. With this money as my ammunition, I secured extra funds from my new acquaintance. Her want to help me was innocent. Her only guilt was by association to a man who had learned a long time ago how to present his potential rather than his limits. Although I had not committed physical adultery, I had strayed away from my family with the justification that it was all for my family! The massive trap had been set.

The hideous four horsemen—terror, bewilderment, frustration, and despair—had once again returned to my daily thoughts. Without the release of alcohol and drugs to relieve—or give the illusion of relief—to my situation, I had no other place to take my frustration except inward. Suicide had again become an alternative in my world of a less-than existence. I had betrayed my best friend with my lack of trust and straying thoughts.

The man I once studied to become fell down, a coward in front of the Devil himself and in shame to the God who allowed this choice. I knew God was still nearby, but I had placed so many obstacles between us that His light could only cast a shadow over the burn I felt.

My terror ripped through everything I had amassed, causing it to crash around me. The money had served only to promote excessive foolishness. My hopes of finally becoming a secure man were soon replaced by broken promises. No longer able to hold onto employment, I was back to being a small child, full of fear, without confidence, ability, or motivation.

I longed for the silence to appear. This time, because God had expelled the Devil from my consciousnesses, I could only hope to leave, to leave as the coward I had become. No longer able to provide for my family, I had lost all dignity as a man to stand next to my wife.

* * *

Weeping, I limped to the Cincinnati Bus Terminal and boarded with the name of another, leaving a note for whoever found my car. Arriving in Albuquerque, I stepped off into a world I had once known. The desert heat and the smell of dirt blowing through the air was small comfort to my new identity. Not knowing how to expunge my previous life, I simply gathered my few belongings and reached for a phonebook and newspaper.

In short order I found an apartment. Tucked back inside an old southeast neighborhood, I was comforted by the bathroom with its working light bulb and flushing toilet. The gap at the bottom of the front door to the two-room

271

efficiency was just enough, I discovered, to let the cool desert air slip in and rob me of my warmth. The cockroaches and other creatures of the night were there to steal any remaining warmth from this weakened body, which hoped only to find the arms of death. Waking the next morning left no doubt that the level of my existence had tumbled as I shook the insects from my hair and arms in what would become a daily ritual.

Scared, and yet somehow released, I found a car dealer who was all too happy to take my five hundred dollars for a broken fog-machine disguised as a car. I drove directly to the only vaguely legitimate local pawnshop and pawned my meager belongings. My goal was to find a casino and escape into a sea of strangers who would not care who I was. That is who I wanted to become: nobody.

After a few weeks, loneliness led to bewilderment. I had secured a position at a local bowling alley to sweep floors for money, under the table. Although the morning insect-shake routine had become almost acceptable, it reminded me daily of what once was and how this life was not what I felt I deserved.

One day I opened the door of my efficiency to a knock. On the other side of the door stood the woman I knew from thousands of miles away. The woman whom I had involved in my Mortal Sin, degraded, and isolated, now stood on my stoop, there to rescue me from my prison of shame. Ecstatic, I threw away my feelings of guilt and accepted the generous effort she extended. She had assumed the role of partner to a fool.

After spending a night without vermin in my bed for the first time in a month, I rested with sound assurances that life may have offered me yet another chapter. After a good meal and conversation, I felt humbled and appreciative. We flew back to Indiana that afternoon.

The next day Patty and I compromised on the solution to settle our affairs. In the weeks before any legal conclusion was determined, we made many attempts made to reignite our love, but there had been too many violations and we had grown too far apart for mending. Once more, basic character flaws and my life's patterns had altered a course of aspiration and hope. My existence in the lake house, where I now resided alone, rested upon a bed of coals.

I had constructed another prison of isolation. My physical conditions were worsening; my mental strength was sapped. I sat in the house I could no longer afford.

Chapter 23

HOPELESS BY DESIGN

If nothing happens in God's world by mistake, then how does God's world allow such strife? Can it really be by design? Is there really a purpose or direction, or is life nothing more than energy that floats by with our vague recognition? I had suffered my whole life from physical pain surpassed only by emotional and mental torment. I found myself still needing to prove my own self-worth, to prove that I had the courage and strength that I was expected to have…to find the "backbone" we *Homo sapiens* are supposed to have. I truly felt that now my life included someone on whom I could rely in the tough days ahead, even in the depths of depression.

Utilizing every skill and bit of knowledge I had, I secured employment once again. After some well-placed name-dropping, I was again making ridiculous sums of money, this time in New England. Ironically, this form of daily entertainment made sense to me and only a few select others.

However, even with the security of being a brother among brothers in a field of focus, my discomfort was transparent. After spending time working in Portland, Maine, it was time to leave, but first I decided to enjoy the summer in the area. Sensing my days were limited, I took a month to dance across the landscape. Each venue offered new smells, sights, and sounds unknown in the heart of the Mid-West.

Eventually I exercised the option to retire. It was a conscious choice to safeguard the remaining short years I might still have before the inevitable began by putting the necessary monetary and medical staples into position.

I would like to say that decision worked to bring about a positive end at this point, but to be honest I would have to say that change, although always present, is not always for the good. As I soon would discover again, changes of great magnitude for me are often mere breaths of doubt to others.

It was on a Tuesday morning, only weeks after leaving a collection of strangers gathered in Northern seclusion, I sipped my java, weighing the pain against the chores ahead.

The television painted an abstract view of a place once seen as a unified pillar: twin towers, both matriarch to those who would rest at her feet and patriarch to New York and the country. The colors began to bleed together, masking a vibrant canvas with illustrations of pain beyond my comprehension. If what I was witnessing were real, what would God in heaven do to correct the scar?

With one swipe of a brush, God's world changed and so did our fears. 9/11 shook me to my core. My failure to live as a man, a son, and father all took a place behind the oily blur that day. I can only assume this was the same emotional reaction Norma once had on that November day in 1963.

For many days my soul wept, as I'm sure did the souls of countless others, in distress as well as with a need for retaliation. I understood emotionally, rather than mentally, for the first time, that it is impossible to be of service to others until we are able to be of service to ourselves.

For me personally, the threads of moral and spiritual cohesion have been regained through forgiveness, of myself and of others, though the integrity

277

of those threads was inherently flawed. Flaws, which perhaps had been instilled into that small isolated coffin of a cast forty-three years ago, were coming ever closer to closing that circle of completion. There would be no more surgeries, no more additions, only extractions now to come. Amputations would soon arrive. Each experience of loneliness and isolated retirement had become confused with golden years of anguish. It would be in these brief years to come that my purpose of helping or serving would be implemented through expressions of color on canvas. "Primitive literalism" is a term that surrounds my senile build-up of paint. Insanity has escaped in times of clarity over the years.

Perhaps my accounting sheds little light on the purpose of my travels. I intend for you to see, to learn how to see, the good in others. When I have been asked to tell about my efforts in this direction, I have hailed away for fear the truth would only reveal the lack of character from which I suffer. I have always been more impressed with your achievements in any comparison with my own. Nor do I choose to expose the faults of another…we are all but human.

Raised by those who tried to be the best they could be, I know that my life stumbled along the most fluid channel available. Somehow I cannot help but feel that my trials may offer you inspiration or insight; certainly I would like to believe that building character through pain and suffering has a certain credibility, a certain truth. But truth is a funny word. I once believed myself to be a truthful person, righteous in my walk, and kind in my giving. But does a person who suffers from self-aggrandizement deserve to be righteous? Do the people who trample across the waves of humanity's goodness without penalty deserve to feel righteous?

My life has been filled with penalties...penalties I suffered for the actions of others as well as my own. Some will say punishment is of our own making and I would have to agree, and the weight of this knowledge I will take with me when I go. Yet I have endured the path, the dusty Midway that existed on trinkets and glitz, and returned to that same illusion over and over in an effort to grab that elusive ring of change, the golden ring to solve my struggles, a reward to counter the penalties of sin.

Forgiveness is only a short grasp away.

I would like to tell you that the past twenty years have culminated into what is now a calm resting place for a wearied soul. Nevertheless, I cannot help think of the lives I have touched, both negatively and positively. If given the chance I would ask the same that was asked of me, "Do you hold anything against me?"

* * *

My father passed away in the same small town where he last lived. After a year or so of not hearing from him, I went to see him. It was during Christmas week, and I had envisioned a strong need to see him. I traveled across those same Indiana roads with guards of wood standing by the road, my heart feeling heavier with each passing mile. A man I barely recognized answered my knock at the door, standing firm against the cold air.

Our conversation went as scripted. I was overwhelmed by the same gray skin I had last seen on my mother. After twenty minutes of rehearsing a play that would never see its curtain rise, I exited as quickly as I had appeared. "Can I do anything for you, Dad?" I asked as I turned to go out the door.

The familiar voice of authority simply replied, "No."

"I love you, Dad," I said. "Please let me know if there's anything I can do."

There was no response and the door closed behind me.

On the drive out of town, through the lone stoplight, I sensed this was my father's last appearance. I called the local sheriff and introduced myself to tell him that should the man they called the "Gray Fox" pass away, I was his only remaining family. On the second day of January, seventy-two hours after I took leave of my father's house, my premonition became a reality.

I was struck by how little I had known of this man, my father. As I cleaned out his house, tucked deep inside a drawer of his bedroom dresser I found a collection of boxes resting quietly next to an empty Rolex case. Inside sat all of my Cub Scout medals, a gathering of tokens from half a century ago. I wondered how many times he had reviewed the contents. His love for me was displayed in isolation, as it always had been.

My life has never gained the glitter I once dreamed it would have. But that's okay. In fact, a quiet, unnoticed exit feels appropriate for a simple man of simple means, alone and absent from all family connections. For my grandchildren whom I know not, I wish a better way.

Twenty plus years of empty life will pass by relatively unnoticed, a lonely walk along the storefront by a darkened, aged man, my stride assisted, mind weakened.

This old house resting upon the hill offers me a view from just across the tracks of that carnival once visited. My pallet is dry now. The colors I see no more. The rain has washed away the signs that once stood for a prosperous home and family. My grave is waiting. The dreams that once filled my head with images of a united world, hope, and companionship for all are gone. The tales spoken through my canvas only draw darker as the years move on to bitter cold nights.

My legs have been gone for years; I know not where they rest. The confines of chafing steel bars rest against my scars at night, nightly horrors of the memories I once escaped. Health lasted a few years once, happiness I cannot remember. All that comes to me now are glimpses of faces that once graced my soul. Faces of hurt remain for hours to challenge my mind with terror. I only hope my final exit gives witness to the beauty I have seen, the beauty of a world that can heal itself through the giving of one to another. To be of use; to want for nothing. That was my goal. I hope I helped.

Silence has arrived many times before tranquility. Silent grace is all I ever asked for in this world of pain. If all of this was by design, I understand not the reason or rhyme or cost. My physical body never complete; my life always wanting for value. Are those more fortunate truly deserving to be the granted patrons of what they receive? The deserving of this world smash the aspirations of the masses without a thought.

Some have said that I carried an "energy of good" about myself in my travels. I too have seen an aura of light around many who have walked beside me. I once considered that my spirit was that of previous life and that reincarnation was possible. If, in fact, reinstatement comes to these who stroll with the spirit, then who is to say you do not come back to the exact position you left? I have often wondered if my body was whole or complete in a life past and, if so, whose life was it?

* * *

This completes the accounting of my life. I hope the veins I explored help guide your thoughts to a place of rest. If not, use the confusion to clear away your own collection of refuse. My words are from the heart. I practice a daily effort to watch for those who among us are in need and wait not for the invitation to help. Please do the same: assist. Participate and gain a connection to another human being.

Through prayer and work our sins can be forgiven and can serve as an accounting if performed in the right spirit. I have chosen to see the good around me. Finding the good is something we can all do, even those who do not have the means to reach. You can serve as the extensions for these people, filling the spaces where emptiness exists.

I can only say this because of what I have learned. My life is blessed and the people around me have found their own blessings. I encourage you: do not let the negative win. The positive force of this earth is far greater than any false image presented.

My journey has been a full, rich experience, and that includes gimping down the road with braces flying and feeling like a misfit in a band of gypsies. Mental and spiritual starvation have given me the opportunity to work on my character and I hope and pray that work never ends. I pray that as I awake each morning in the palm and cradle of a loving God, His warmth forgives my errors. I no longer seek escape.

I have no explanations for my visions, other than to tell you I try each day to engage and live in a spiritual world. Religion plays little if any role in my life because of man's failure to represent the true principles of God. I live a life of abstinence with few worldly pleasures. I am often afraid of what this life will yield before it is over. It is my deep and sincere desire to pass from this world with the quietest of farewells.

Please do not ask me to argue my case. I know only the life I have lived. I do not claim to be knowledgeable in anything other than that.

One last observation, if you will indulge me.

If you have ever wondered about another human who is different from you in appearance, try to find the similarities, not the differences. We are more alike than we are different.

This is my first attempt at writing for the purposes of documenting my life. Perhaps it will not be my last. Time will tell, as it always does.

Thank you, and God bless. I hope your journey is a humble one.

ABOUT THE AUTHOR

As an artist in spirit and gift, Kris Courtney has lived much of his life in the Midwest and currently resides near his studio in Oxford Ohio. Surrounded by talent and gifted students of life, daily affairs are comprised of service and volunteer work. A percentage of the earnings from this book will go to research for Parkinson's disease and Colon Cancer in recognition of the illnesses that attacked his grandmother Flossie and his mother, Norma Jean.

Norma Jean's Sun is Kris Courtney's tribute to a mother that sacrificed everything for her severely crippled son. Courtney is an artist in both paint and words. In his touching memoir, he captures the essence of a tragic life and the beauty that lies beneath the surface. His words paint a picture of a hardship and a suffering that only few could imagine. Using a painters brush, Courtney scratches out his emotional story in an abstraction of language that parallels a life that just will not give up. As his mother told him many times, this remarkably talented man continues to fight.

57740994R00160

Made in the USA
Charleston, SC
21 June 2016